Richard M. Raichelson

Beale Street Talks

A Walking Tour Down the Home of the Blues

Beale Street Talks: A Walking Tour Down the Home of the Blues
Copyright ©1999 Richard M. Raichelson
Library of Congress Catalog Card Number: 98-73840

ISBN 0-9647545-1-7

Computerization and Formatting: James M. Doran
Cover Design and Maps: Dana Gregory and Wayne Tregler
Photography: Evanne Newman, Renee Graham-Castleberry, and Robert T. Jones

Special Acknowledgment to:
Mrs. Leo Brody, William Day, John Dougan, Dr. Bobbie Flannery and the staff of the Memphis/Shelby Co. Archives, Ed Frank, Jim Hickman, Dr. Jim Johnston and the staff of the Memphis/Shelby Co. Room, Doris Lee, David Less, Perre Magness, Gene Miller, Rufus Thomas, and Ernest C. Withers

Photograph Credits:
Memphis Room, Memphis and Shelby County Library-pages 3, 5, 6, 10, 11, 14, 15, 18, 21, 23, 24, 25, 27, 29, 31, 33, 35, 37, 38, 39, 41, 45, 47, 49, 55, 59, 61, 69, 75, 76, 80, 81, 83, 85, 87, 90, 92, 93, 95, 96, 98, 99
Memphis Music & Blues Museum, Inc./Hooks Brothers Photography Collection-pages 17, 26, 32, 42, 53, 62, 66, 71, 79
Mississippi Valley Collection-pages 16, 54, 78
Arcadia Archive-pages 1 (facing page), 7, 19, 43, 46, 51, 57, 58, 63, 70, 72, 73, 108
Robert T. Jones Archive-pages 40, 50
Margaret Skinner-page 67

Cover Photograph: Beale Street looking east from Hernando (Rufus Thomas Blvd.), ca. 1915.

Second, Revised Edition

For additional copies write:
Arcadia Records
P.O. Box 240544
Memphis, TN 38124

CONTENTS

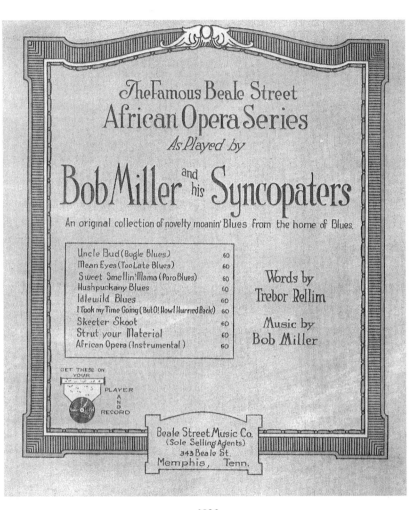

1923

INTRODUCTION

Beale Street, running west from the Mississippi River to its easternmost boundary near the University of Tennessee Medical Center, is only one-and-one-half miles long. Most know about Beale from its position in the annals of American music, where it has earned the title "Home of the Blues," and is recognized as the place which W. C. Handy immortalized in his song "Beale Street Blues." Music is the mystique of Beale; the glue which binds it to history and attracts thousands of visitors each year.

But the sound of so many black and blue chords and rhythms do not tell the complete story. Nor do the survivors of urban renewal: a small number of brick and cast-iron store fronts which look like trees lining a path cut through an open meadow. If Beale Street could talk, it would chatter about its heyday when its sidewalks and cobblestone streets were gorged with traffic; when its curbs and those of its cross streets were packed full of all kinds of homes, businesses, churches, professional offices, and entertainment facilities; when it served a large, vibrant, and multicultural community which became increasingly African-American over its life span of one hundred plus years.

In the 1840s Beale Street was part of South Memphis which included a large area south of Union Avenue. Union represented the dividing line between Memphis and its fledgling rival. Both towns were consolidated in January 1850. Robertson Topp, a Memphis attorney, entrepreneur, and the founder of South Memphis, gave the street its name in honor of an American military hero.

In the beginning, especially at its eastern end, Beale was a suburb for the affluent. There is only one mansion left: the Hunt-Phelan Home. During this period a number of businesses were established in the western part of the street. In the 1850s a small number of free blacks settled in this area but, during the Civil War, the African-American population grew from the influx of contraband, freedmen, and black Union troops.

On 1 May 1866 a bloody race riot occurred, sparked by an altercation between black Union troops and the police, over 80 percent of whom were Irish. The actual cause was due to a long-standing economic competition between the African-American and Irish populations, the dislike of Memphians for Unionism, and the social threat felt by the city over the influx of thousands of blacks during the Civil War.

At the time, several thousand black Union troops and their families were living in contraband camps in the southern part of Memphis and at Fort Pickering, around eight blocks south of Beale. On April 30th, the troops were mustered out of the army and some 150 of them decided to celebrate in the saloons around Fourth and Calhoun. A number of Memphis police made an attempt to arrest one of them who had a run-in with four officers the previous day. Shots were fired and the police retreated north to Beale and Main Street where the battle ended. But that night and over the next couple of days, the police and a white posse descended on the area to burn and loot scores of homes, schools, and churches. As the crowd shoved its way south, they also indiscriminately beat and shot black residents who lived around Beale. Although hundreds of blacks fled Memphis, by the 1870s a sizeable population remained in the vicinity of Beale Street.

A series of yellow fever epidemics in the 1870s devastated the city, especially in 1878. In August of that year, when the first impact of the disease was felt, 25,000 inhabitants fled the city in a two-week period. They left behind relief workers, medical personnel, and a remaining population of 20,000 which consisted mostly of poor Memphians: around 14,000 African-Americans and several thousand Irish. From the middle of August to the middle of October, there were 17,600 cases, 5,150 of whom died. Blacks, relatively immune to the worst ravages of the disease, accounted for 12,000 cases, but only 946 or 7 percent died.

The African-American population around Beale Street helped to manage the city, care for the sick, and bury the dead. Two black militia groups, the Zouave Guard and the McClellan Guard, assisted in protecting residents from looters and total chaos.

The Yellow Fever Epidemic of 1878 ruined local businesses and added to the city debt which had been rising during the 1870s. Memphis forfeited its charter in 1879 and it became a taxing district of the state. In 1881 the city issued municipal bonds to reestablish its charter. Robert Church, Sr., a black businessman, bought the first one for one thousand dollars. During the 1870s, Church purchased land around Beale Street which eventually made him a millionaire.

In the 1880s and 1890s, with the emergence of a small black middle class, an independent and viable African-American community began to take shape in the Beale Street area between Second Street and Wellington (now, Danny Thomas Boulevard). African-Americans became established in various businesses which grew in number after the turn of the century.

Nevertheless from the nineteenth and well into the twentieth century, many whites lived and owned businesses in the neighborhood. Jews owned pawnshops, clothing, and department stores; Italians operated saloons, theaters, and grocery stores; Greeks ran restaurants; Chinese managed laundries and restaurants; there were Irish, German, and French merchants.

Cotton being loaded onto the Ferd Herald, Memphis riverfront, 1900. The Ferd Herald was part of the Memphis-based Lee Line and, for most of its thirty years on the river, traveled between Memphis and St. Louis.

In the 1900s a significant number of black professionals, businessmen, and landowners were present, such as physicians, dentists, lawyers, pharmacists, restaurant owners, tailors, photographers, undertakers, teachers, barbers, and real estate brokers. African-Americans owned newspapers, banks, hotels, life insurance companies, saloons, fraternal clubs and societies, churches, entertainment agencies, and various mercantile establishments, such as clothing stores, jewelry shops, and beauty salons. Beale Street was the center for black social and civic activities, including church and political conventions, school proms, club gatherings, the Cotton Makers Jubilee (the black version of a carnival saluting the role of cotton in the economy of Memphis), and the Civil Rights Movement.

In addition to Beale Street, other major black residential and business enclaves existed in South and North Memphis, Orange Mound, Binghampton, and in Hollywood, among others. But Beale Street was the hub of social, civic, and business activity for blacks not only in Memphis but in the entire Mid-South.

Arkansas farmers, during the nineteenth century, were brought by ferryboat directly to the foot of Beale to do their Saturday shopping. In the mid-1880s the first thing they saw, as they unloaded their horses and wagons, was the small levee home of Robert D. Lee, a sanitary policeman (a health inspector). Moving up Beale, they passed Jackson Halstead's fish depot, the black tenement which was home to fisherman Luke Ward and fireman John Ragan, and the saloons of E. M. Castagnino and Stephen Cuneo. As they crossed Front Street, George Gabray's variety store, Lewis Arnold's news shop, or J. Raines' barbershop may have perked their interest. On the southside of the block, C. B. Bryan's huge soot-infested wood and coal yard accompanied them before they reached Main Street. On the northeast corner of Beale and Main, the stately Second Presbyterian Church cast a respectable shadow over Andrew Garibaldi's diminutive drinking establishment which stood on the southeast corner. As their wagon wheels banged loudly against cobblestones, they passed by Charley Kney's meat market, Angus Campbell's grocery, a building shared by Justice's Feed Store and the saloon of Josh Sartore, and before reaching the corner of Beale and Second, the Fahlen and Kleinschmidt Drug Store. Going north on Second for one-half a block, they arrived at Keck's Livery Stable where they could board their horses and wagons. Next door was a horse-shoeing and blacksmith shop and a mule shed; across the street the Central Baptist Church. From this vantage point, they were within three blocks of most businesses in the area.

Everyday life on Beale from the late 1800s through the first half of the 1900s, was a reoccurring drama played-out as street theater. Saturdays, especially, jumped with activity. In the daytime, the crowded levee overflowed with riverboats, roustabouts, bales of cotton and other goods, various hucksters and vendors, as well as an assortment of characters who frequented the nearby saloons and cafés. Further east on Beale, sidewalks were filled with displays of clothes, racks of shoes, stacks of watermelon, and swarms of people. Pullers hovered in front of pawn shops and dry goods stores trying to attract customers. Peddlers pushed their carts as they began their rounds. The street had fortune tellers, herb doctors, and even gadgets like the lung-testing machine where for a nickel customers could check their lung power by blowing through a rubber tube. The smell of fried food, fresh vegetables and meats, and the rotting odor of fish pierced the air. Street vendors sold tamales and fried catfish, while hucksters hawked fruit with high-pitched cries. In later years Tony's Fruit Stand and Joe Spinoza's fruit wagon became institutions. Farmers with produce to sell, like vegetables, eggs, or chickens, parked their wagons somewhere on Beale or next to the Market House.

The Market House was torn down in 1930 to make way for Handy Park which was perfectly located near businesses, clubs, and the theater district. It became an open-air meeting hall for the community and echoed with the polyphonic din of the crowd, the rhythmic pulse of preachers and bluesmen, as well as the awkward shuffle of winos, sounds which staggered into the evening hours.

After dark, the attention of the crowd shifted to the theaters, dance halls, and restaurants which lit up the street with a steady stream of bright multicolored lights. Slick and rough-and-tumble hustlers moved in and out of the Hole in the Wall, Midway, and Panama, three of Beale's numerous gambling lairs. The Chop Suey, New York, and New Orleans Cafés braced for the onslaught of dinner-time patrons and waited eagerly for the after-theater crowd. The Avalon, Monarch, and Rex pool rooms cracked with the snap of cue sticks and billiard balls. Shadowy bordellos, on Third and Fourth Streets, switched on their porch lights (white patrons had their emporiums just one block north on Gayoso). Night life on Beale was exciting, some of

Peddlers wagon, Handy Park, ca. 1940.

it deviant and dangerous, but typical of any place which concentrated an assortment of characters, easy money, and booze.

Amid the hubbub and bustle of night life, music filled the air between Third Street and Danny Thomas Boulevard, as well as up and down cross streets. Itinerant blues musicians and the popular jug bands played for handouts on street corners and in Handy Park. Blues combos and pianists pounded out their rhythms in seedy smoke-filled clubs and in the many rough gambling dens. Jazz orchestras performed for dances, dinners, and proms, in Church Park Auditorium, in nightclubs and theaters, and for the many fraternal organizations, such as the Elks Club and Masonic Lodge.

As if to keep everything honest and in balance, gospel music rose from the pulpits and pews of both storefront and larger churches, such as

Centennial Baptist and Union Grove Baptist Church. Two of them, Avery Chapel and First Baptist Beale Street Church, were only a few doors away from Beale and Fourth, the intersection that was home to some of the most notorious gambling and drinking spots on the street. The proximity of such conflicting images all contributed to the energy, vitality, and fame of Beale Street. Although little of it remains physically, there is still much to talk about.

Ad for The Southern Hotel (current #: 70 Beale), 1899

Ad for Jackson Halstead, fish depot, 1893.

"The Jogo Blues," an instrumental piece published in 1913 by W. C. Handy. It furnished the famous chorus for the "St. Louis Blues."

MODERN BEALE STREET

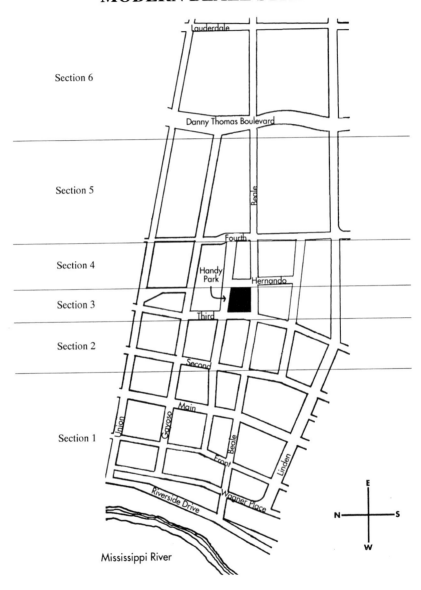

HOW TO USE THIS TOUR GUIDE

In 1966 Beale Street was placed on the national register of historic places. Eventually, this came to include only those blocks between Second and Fourth Street. From 1969 until the early 1970s, the street and its surrounding environs underwent extensive urban renewal in which hundreds of buildings were demolished. For the most part, Beale Street as an established community disappeared by 1970. Consequently, many of the buildings discussed in this guide are no longer in existence.

The **FORMAT** for each building listed is:
1. Name of building or primary occupant.
2. Current occupant, if different, in parentheses.
3. Architect of building, if known.
4. Date of construction.
5. Original street number, if any.
6. Description of original occupancy and architecture of building; narrative of people and events, where appropriate.

Note: Although current occupancy may change, it is accurate as of July 1999. The original street numbers may not exactly match current ones. In 1904 Memphis changed its numbering system to keep pace with city growth. Many of the ads in this book were from the 1800s with numbers that reflect the old method. Where appropriate, the modern number is given in parentheses.

This guide contains an overview map of modern Beale Street and six sectional maps which show how Beale looked in the 1930s. These maps cover a distance of one-and-one-fifth miles from the riverfront east to Beale and Lauderdale.

Section 1: The Riverfront to Second Street - includes the Orpheum Theater.
Section 2: Second Street to Third Street - main business district.
Section 3: Third Street to Hernando (Rufus Thomas Blvd) - Handy Park area.
Section 4: Hernando to Fourth Street - theater district.
Section 5: Fourth Street to Turley (This street no longer goes through to Beale) - Church Park District.
Section 6: Danny Thomas Boulevard to Lauderdale - mansion district.

WALKING THE TOUR

It is recommended that the walking tour begin with the Orpheum Theater (Section 1), Main and Beale, and end at Church Park (Section 5), east of Fourth Street. For distances east of Church Park, a car is recommended. Each section is arranged so that the walk from the Orpheum Theater to Church Park can be made on either the north or south side of Beale. In fact, the tour may begin anywhere on the map and even in the other direction by simply reversing the way the book is read. The numerical sequencing of buildings, in most cases, alternates even (northside) with odd (southside) street numbers.

Ad for John Oakey, liquor dealer (current #: 203 Beale), 1882.

The Memphis levee, ca. 1891. At the lower left: The Newport News and Mississippi Valley Railroad (later the Illinois Central) freight depot; a coal chute leading down to barges; on the bluff, the Gayoso House, a hotel. At the right: The steeple of the Pittsburgh Coal Company elevator; the back of the newly built Grand Opera House; the Valley Oil Mills Company nearly hanging over the bluff. Beale is the muddy-looking road in the middle, parallel to the coal chute.

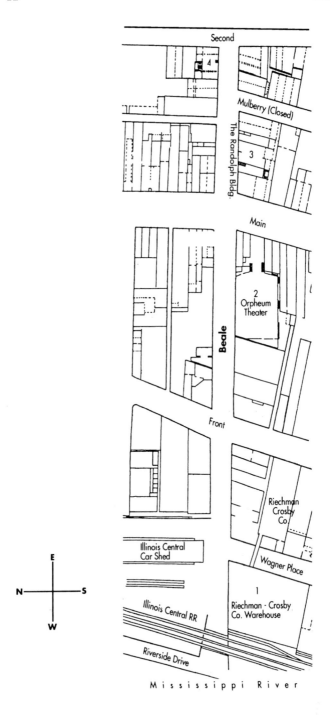

The Riverfront to Second Street

SECTION 1
THE RIVERFRONT TO SECOND STREET

1. THE RIECHMAN-CROSBY CO. WAREHOUSE
(No. 1 Beale)
ca.1921
SW corner Beale and Wagner Place

During the 1880s, this was the location of several coal firms, including from 1890 to l921, a branch office of the Pittsburgh Coal Company (see photo on page 15).

The warehouse was built for the Riechman-Crosby Company, at the time the largest mill and factory supply outlet in the South. Many features of the building remain unaltered, including an unusual pitched roof and large window openings. Three large loading docks faced the railroad tracks on the west. An overhead walkway across Wagner Place connected the warehouse to the main offices on Front Street, both now demolished. The company moved in the 1950s.

From 1921 to 1922, Riechman-Crosby owned WKN, the first commercial radio station in Memphis. The company sold its channel to the Commercial Appeal, a local newspaper, which began broadcasting in January 1923 as WMC. It is still in operation.

2. THE ORPHEUM THEATER
Rapp and Rapp, Chicago, Architects
1928
SW corner Beale and Main

In the late 1840s, grocer William McKeon built a ten room house on this site. Its marble fireplace mantels and mahogany furniture were matched by beautifully landscaped grounds which included gardens, flowers, and fruit trees. A cistern was built to contain up to 400 barrels of water. The family remained at this location until the late 1860s. Sometime in the early 1880s, the house was replaced by the C. B. Bryan Wood and Coal Yard which, in turn, was razed in 1889 to make way for the Grand Opera House (see photo).

Fitted with a facade of blue or bluff stone, the opera house opened on 22 September 1890 with a production of *Les Huggenots*. The Grand was regarded as the finest and most elegant theater outside New York City. The Chickasaw Guards, a nationally recognized military unit of the Tennessee

National Guard, used the opera house as their headquarters. The upper floors became the Chickasaw Club where the elite of Memphis dined and danced.

In 1899 Colonel John D. Hopkins of Louisville bought the theater and, under the management of A. B. Morrison, changed the format to include vaudeville performances between the acts of dramatic plays. The Orpheum Vaudeville Theater Circuit purchased the building in 1907. Some of the great artists who performed were Sarah Bernhardt, Lillian Russell, and Ignace Jan Paderewski.

The predecessor of the Orpheum Theater: The Grand Opera House, 1895.

On the evening of 16 October 1923, a fire broke out in the Tri-State Manufacturing Company, a maker of women's dresses. This business occupied the third floor of the theater facing Beale. As musicians frantically grabbed their instruments and actors hastily stuffed their wardrobe trunks, the ceiling fell onto the stage lighting up the scenery in a ball of flame. The next morning the hollow walls of the theater strained to support the marquee which reached out to passersby in disbelief. On the bill was the great vaudevillian Blossom Seeley, who lost several thousand dollars worth of scenery and wardrobe.

The Memphis Theater and Realty Company raised $750,000 to rebuild the theater but it ended up costing $1.6 million. The theater took one year to build and opened on 19 November 1928, under RKO management, with Rae Samuels, the "Blue Streak of Vaudeville." The new Orpheum could seat 2,800. It showed films and booked nationally known vaudeville acts and topnotch orchestras, including Bob Hope, Mae West, the Ink Spots, Jack Benny, and the orchestras of Duke Ellington, Cab Calloway, Louis Armstrong, and Paul Whiteman. Stage shows and dramatic plays also were scheduled, such as *Shanghai Nights* and *Tobacco Road.*

In 1934 the Orpheum tested the Tennessee blue laws which made it a criminal act to show films on Sunday. The owners, the Chicago Theater Company, backed manager Charles Mensing in instituting Sunday "Sandwich Shows" where patrons paid forty cents for a sandwich and a soft drink but saw the film for free. Supported by Congressman Edward H. Crump, other Memphis theaters, and the general public, film showings on Sunday were legalized.

After several changes of ownership and years of neglect, the Memphis Development Foundation restored the theater to its original condition. It reopened in 1984. Enlargement of the stage and additional rennovations were made in 1997.

Ad for A. Hunn and Company (current #: 156 Beale), 1866.

3. THE RANDOLPH BUILDING
(Elvis Presley Plaza - original building demolished)
1891
SE corner Beale and Main

The Randolph Building, ca. 1910. Note the trolleys in the foreground, a form of transportation which has returned to Main Street in Memphis.

Samuel McManus, who was a wholesale dealer in stoves, grates, and all types of metal ware, built a home on this site in the 1840s. His son, James C. McManus, was a steamboat captain and later an auctioneer. In the 1880s Andrew Garibaldi operated a saloon in the building which was one of several structures torn down to accomodate the Randolph Office Building.

Named for lawyer William M. Randolph, the Randolph Office Building stood on land now occupied by the Elvis Presley statue and the Memphis Light, Gas, and Water Company. The finest and largest office building in the city during the 1890s, the Randolph Building had seven stories, 240 offices, and its own water supply drawn from an artesian well dug 400 feet through the basement. Constructed of brick and iron, the design was from the Florentine Renaissance. William Randolph and his two sons had their law offices in the building. The Randolph Mansion, also in this guide, stood a few blocks east at 546 Beale (building #56).

4. LANSKY BROTHERS UNIFORM SHOP/BLUE LIGHT PHOTOGRAPHY STUDIO
(Elvis Presley's Memphis)
late 1860s
126-128/130 Beale

Lansky Brothers was originally to the left of the Mississippi River Café. Photo from around 1950.

Although this building currently has a single address, 126 Beale, it originally consisted of three separate stores. Between 1900 and World War II, 126-128 Beale contained secondhand clothing, furniture, restaurant, and shoe repair businesses. Beginning as a uniform store in 1946, Lansky Brothers (126-128 Beale) became famous for being clothier to Elvis Presley. Other stars also shopped there, including Jerry Lee Lewis, Carl Perkins, B. B. King, Bobby "Blue" Bland, and Rufus Thomas. Lansky gave Thomas free suits for advertising his store. When Rufus appeared on the stage of the Handy Theater, he opened his coat and shouted, "Ain't I'm clean? You know who makes me clean?" The audience screamed back, "Lansky Brothers!"

In 1942 the Blue Light Photography Studio occupied the corner of this building (130 Beale). In the early 1960s, it became part of Lansky Brothers Big and Tall Men's Shop. Prior to World War II, the building was used mostly as a restaurant. Thomas Pappas operated one from around 1919 to 1940, usually under the workingman's trademark, Joe's Lunch Room.

About 75 feet west of this building was the first location of the Freedmen's Savings and Trust Bank (120 Beale), opened in 1866 by the Federal Government to serve the huge black population which had grown in Memphis during the Civil War. In 1874 it became Charley Kney's market, a dealer in meats, fish, and game.

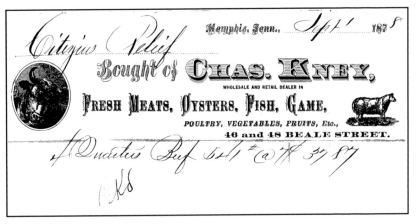

Invoice from Charley Kney's market (current #: 120 Beale) to Citizen's Relief, 1878. Citizen's Relief was organized by the city to help those in times of need, in this case the yellow fever epidemic of 1878.

Ad for Orpheum Theater, 1937.

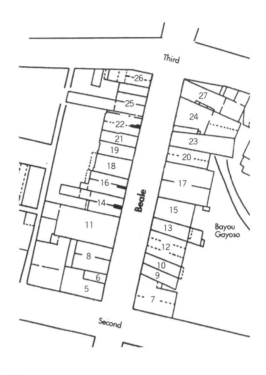

Second Street to Third Street

SECTION 2
SECOND STREET TO THIRD STREET

5. CAPITAL LOANS
(Blues City Café)
ca. 1927
138 Beale

Capital Loans, early 1970s.

Although this building may have been built during the 1880s, it was significantly altered around 1927 to accomodate one of Clarence Saunders' Piggly Wiggly Stores. Saunders has been credited with developing the first self-serve grocery store.

In 1891 the first of several proprietors operated saloons at this location until the late 1910s. One of them, Michael Dicicco, also owned a grocery store and became a partner in the National Sales and Exchange Company which dealt in real estate, merchandise, and even stocks.

In 1895 and for the next fifteen years, one part of this building contained Justices of the Peace and deputy sheriffs. In 1934 Frank Boro's Sandwich Shop moved in. The Boro Family had owned the property as early as 1854. The business changed to Samuel Angel's pawn shop in 1937 with Capital Loans being the final proprietor in the early 1950s.

6. SAM SALKY, shoe repair
(Blues City Café)
1880s
140 Beale

This small two-story building, with only an eighteen foot frontage, may have been a private residence at one time. From 1886 to 1891 Leopold Horn lived upstairs above his tailor shop. With his two brothers, Abraham and Harry, he became a clothing manufacturer and left Beale around 1892 for larger quarters on Main Street where Peabody Place is now located. Meyer B. Price opened his shoe manufacturing shop here in 1896 and for a few years had a second store a block away. Unlike other businessmen, he never lived on the premise. The Boro Family, owners of the building, rented out the second floor as living quarters to Antonio Nuvolini and other owners of the saloon next door at 138 Beale (building #5). Price's store closed around 1908. Later occupants included other shoemakers, clothing stores, a jewelry company, and it was the first location of Capital Loans. The last occupant, from the mid-1950s until urban renewal, was Mrs. Mattie Pegue's coffee shop.

Morris Salky, shoemaker, was here briefly from 1915 to 1917 before he moved to South Main to open a clothing and tailoring business with his brother Max. They were at 518 S. Main Street through the 1950s which is currently the home of WEVL-Fm 90 Community Radio. Morris' son, Sam, had a shoe repair shop for years at another location before he settled in at 140 Beale from 1933 until the late 1940s. He then quit the shoe business and became a salesman at Jack and Herman Salky's pawn shop, 122 Beale.

7. FRED L. SCHWANTZ/SIGMUND FEDER
grocery/clothing
(B. B. King's Club)
1924
139-145 Beale

This building was constructed in 1924 due to an alteration in the street. As a result the buildings which housed F. L. Schwantz and Company (grocers and dealers in cigars and tobacco) and S. Feder Brothers (clothing) were torn down. Both businesses had been at their original location since 1896. However, they continued their enterprises in the new building. Schwantz went out of business in 1935, being replaced by the Dixie Liquor Store, while the Feder Brothers continued at the same location until the early 1950s.

Fred L. Schwantz, grocers, occupied the corner section (139 Beale); Sigmund Feder, clothing, the middle two addresses (141 and 143 Beale). The entrance to the second floor was through the door on the far left (145 Beale). Photo from the early 1970s.

After construction of the new building, black physicians, dentists, lawyers, and insurance and real estate agents, among others, had offices on the second floor. Beginning in 1944, the second floor was referred to as the "Colored Business Exchange Building."

8. LERNER BUILDING
(Blues City Café/Blues City General Store)
ca. 1900
142-144 Beale

Although the upper facade of this building indicates that it was constructed in 1924, the date is actually the year the third floor was removed. The building is named for Louis Lerner who purchased the property in 1919. Lerner also owned 174 Beale (building #25).

The west side of the building (142 Beale) housed Joseph Schatz's wholesale clothing business (1909-1928), Samuel Angel's pawn shop (1929-1937), and the Art Hutkin Sales Store (1944-1959). Nathan Novick's Empire Jewelry Store moved in around 1966 and remained open until 1981. Previously, Novick had been at 131 Beale since 1932.

Businesses at 144 Beale (east side of building) included: The Kentucky Supply Company (1906-1916), a liquor store; Jacob Angel (1924-1931) and Joseph Safferstone (1932-1945), both clothing stores; and (Harry) Cohen's Loan Office, from around 1950 until 1973.

A hotel, named Hotel Clark for most of its existence, operated out of

The Lerner Building, early 1970s. Note the entranceway to Hotel Jackson on the second floor.

the second floor from 1925 until the 1960s. From the early 1930s until after World War II, it was a popular stopover for visiting jazz musicians, such as Count Basie. Bands rehearsed in one of the rooms which also hosted frequent after-hours jam sessions.

9. THE VOGUE SHOP, women's clothing
(B. B. King's Gift Shop)
1950s
147 Beale

The top two floors of the original structure, built before 1890, were removed in the 1950s. Jacob Rudner operated his dry goods store at this location from 1906 until 1925. Other occupants were Lester's Women's Clothing (1937-1951) and, beginning in 1952, The Vogue Shop, a women's clothing store owned by Irvin Lansky.

Left to right: Simon Cohen and Sons (149 Beale) and the Vogue Shop (147 Beale). The photo, taken in the early 1970s, shows a hardware store in 149 Beale operated by Art Hutkin.

10. SIMON COHEN AND SONS, dry goods
(Memphis Music - Records, Tapes and Souvenirs)
1880s
149 Beale

Simon Cohen bought this building (see photo for building #9) to house his dry goods store which stayed in operation from the early 1920s through the late 1940s. Prior to this period, it was the original location of Schwab's. In the 1960s Art Hutkin's hardware store became its sole occupant.

At various times rooms were rented for residents and professional offices. Dr. J. C. Hairston moved his medical practice here in 1917 from 323-327 Beale where he remained until the mid-1930s (also see building #36).

The building has a nineteenth-century flavor with its attic vents, slightly arched brick supports above the windows, and cast-iron support columns.

11. ROSENBAUM AND MENDEL, furniture
(Midtown Mental Health Center)
1895
146-152 Beale

Originally a two-story building with the third floor added sometime after 1907, it was the retail outlet of the Morris Rosenbaum and Ike Mendel Furniture Company from 1896 to 1915. The store manufactured furniture in their annex on Second Street, just around the corner from Beale. The Rosenbaum family came to Memphis from Cincinnati in the late 1860s to open a stove and tinware business. In 1918 Rosenbaum left the furniture business to become a partner in a saloon which, under the name "Locker Club," had the distinction of becoming the first speakeasy in Memphis.

Subsequent businesses were usually furniture and clothing stores. The original stairway to the upper floors stood just to the left of the center of the

Left to right: Rosenbaum and Mendel (146-152 Beale), the Watson Building (154-156 Beale), Joseph Morat (158-160 Beale), ca. 1949.

building (see photo). Up these stairs were the display rooms/warehouses of many businesses, such as the Hunt Brothers Furniture Company, Ferguson's Bargain House, and Kiersky's Trading Post which sold store fixtures.

One of these, the Trojan Luggage Company, became an important Memphis business, eventually employing around 700 workers. The founder, Leo Brody, had been a salesman at Epstein's Loan Office (building #18). Around 1940 he opened Brody's, a pawnshop, and in 1946, the Trojan Luggage Company which manufactured foot lockers and trunks. Within a year,

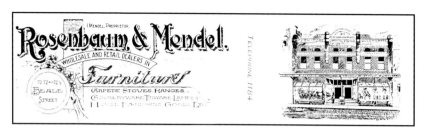

Ad for Rosenbaum and Mendel Furniture Company (current #: 146-152 Beale), 1899.

the firm moved from Beale Street to larger quarters and began to make full three-piece sets of luggage. The company, after further expansion, eventually went out of business in the early 1990s.

The facade of the building has simple but appealing lines and ornamentation. A small cast-iron cap, similar to the one on 162 Beale, once adorned the top of the building. In 1974 about 35 feet were removed from the back portion.

12. GOODMAN BUILDING
(The Black Diamond/Tater Red's Lucky Mojos)
ca. 1938
151-153-155 Beale

Originally, two nineteenth-century three-story buildings stood at this

Left to right: Peter Rendos (157 Beale) the Goodman Building (151-153-155 Beale), ca. 1970.

location. Around 1938 three single-story structures replaced them. These buildings contained such businesses as Ray's Smart Shoes (151 Beale), Paul's Fashion Shop (153 Beale), and the Little Hot House, a restaurant (155 Beale). Abe Goodman, Jr., the owner and probably builder, was the son of Abe Goodman, a well-known Memphis businessman, banker, real estate developer, and civic leader.

13. PETER RENDOS, restaurant
(building demolished)
1880s
157 Beale

Originally a three-story building with the top floor removed in the 1950s (see photo for building #12), it was razed in the 1970s. The site is now a favorite short cut from Beale to the parking lot behind Schwab's. One of the longest on the street, the building was quite narrow in the front but flared-out toward the rear.

Peter Rendos ran a resturant here from 1932 until he retired in 1945. Other businesses were mostly clothing and dry goods stores. Mrs. Pauline Heilpern and her family, before leaving town in 1906, briefly operated a combination grocery/feed store and saloon for thirsty shoppers.

There were several physician, dentist, and legal offices on the second floor, while the third was reserved for residents. Dr. Isaac A. Watson's dental office served the public from 1926 to 1943 (also see building #14).

14. WATSON BUILDING
(Psychics of Beale St./Willis' Gallery)
early 1870s
154-156 Beale

In 1943 a plain brick wall with the inscription, "Watson 1943," replaced the original neoclassical cornice at the top of this building (see photo for building #11). Perhaps the original portion had deteriorated beyond repair, but it is more probable that the new owners, dentists Isaac A. Watson and William H. Young, were in the mood for remodeling their recent acquisition. Dr. Watson had been a highly respected professional on Beale since the mid-1920s. Along with Young, he occupied the second floor until the late 1960s.

Over the years, the first floor of both 154 and 156 Beale contained clothing, pawn, shoe repair, restaurant, and photography businesses, and the Tyler Barber School.

15. PAPE'S MEN'S SHOP
(Police Station)
ca. 1947
159-161 Beale

In 1943 Sigfried Pape bought the nineteenth-century three-story building which originally stood at this location, razed it, and built the current structure. Pape's Men's Shop, the only occupant through the 1960s, sold high quality clothes. The store had an arrangement with the American Finishing Company, a finisher of cotton materials. When one of their employees had an outstanding account with Pape's, the company garnisheed his wages to pay the bill.

From 1906 to 1915, this was the location of the Terrell-Patterson Infirmary. Dr. C. A. Terrell, originally from Alabama, and his nephew, Dr. L. G. Patterson, eventually moved across the street to 164 Beale (building #18). Impressed by the work of Dr. J. C. Hairston's hospital (see building #36), Dr. Terrell founded the Jane Terrell Baptist Hospital and Nursing School in 1912 at 698 Williams Avenue.

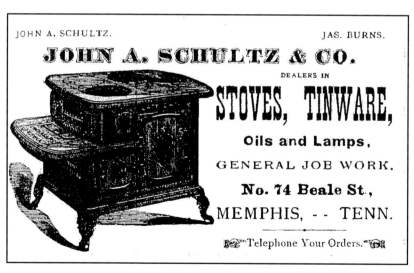

Ad for John A. Schultz and Company (current #: 154 Beale), 1881.

16. JOSEPH MORAT, bakery
(King's Palace Patio - original building demolished)
ca. 1895
158/160 Beale

The building may be seen at the far right in the photo for building #11. Currently, the space is a small but pleasant park and is used by King's Palace Café for outdoor entertainment.

Both Joseph Morat's father, William, and brother, Frederick, were bakers. In 1906 Joseph, with partner William Winkelman, took over the confectionary business founded by Frank Bensieck at 182 Beale (building #26). Morat, as sole proprietor, operated the bakery from 1909 until 1920 when he relocated at 158 Beale (west side of building). Upon his death in 1930, the business closed, but the Home Bakery, William White's Bakery, and Sue's Bakery continued the tradition of baking into the 1960s.

The occupants of 160 Beale (east side of building) included: David Ostrich and Company, pawnbrokers; Samuel Haimsohn, clothier; C. B. Brooks' tailor shop; and Samuel Finklestein's shoe repair shop.

On the second floor, from 1919 to 1947, were the medical offices of Dr. Arthur T. Martin. In 1929 Martin and his three brothers, Drs. William S., a physician, B. B., a dentist, and John B., a pharmacist, gained control of the Memphis Red Sox, a black professional baseball team. The team was founded in 1919 by A. P. Martin (no relation; see building #45). Later on the brothers built a new stadium. B. B. became general manager, while John graduated to the presidency of the Negro American League. Following a dispute with Memphis political boss Edward H. Crump, John relocated to Chicago.

17. A. SCHWAB'S, dry goods
ca. 1865
163-165 Beale

In 1912 Abraham Schwab moved his dry goods business from 149 into larger quarters at 163 Beale. The family business had been on Beale Street since 1876, first as grocers then as dry goods merchants. I. Goldsmith and Brothers, predecessor to the Goldsmith Department Store empire, and L. Bauer and Sons (both dry goods businesses), and then a Piggly Wiggly grocery store occupied 165 Beale until Schwab took over the building in 1924.

Schwab's is the only original business still in operation on the street. Inside and out, it is a remarkable holdover from old Beale Street. The iron

A. Schwab's, 1910s.

attic vents and architectural design is brought out by the deep rich color of the red brick. The interior has high ceilings, wood floors, antiquated display bins, and a variety of merchandise which recall the old-time dry goods store. The photograph shows the original store front with an overhang that extended to the curb to protect customers from bad weather, a common feature during this period.

18. EPSTEIN'S LOAN OFFICE
(King's Palace Café)
1894
162-164 Beale

Epstein's Loan Office, upper portion, early 1970s.

This stylish building features a cast-iron store front, a stone arch over the middle second story window, a carved stone parapet, a classical type of cornice, and a cast-iron cap at its apex. Originally, the building had bay windows set off by the same type of carved stone as the parapet, as well as an overhang located just below the second story window.

Prior to 1920 its businesses included dealers in furniture, dry goods, women's clothing, and hardware. Around 1928 William Epstein opened his loan office which operated at this location through the 1960s.

From the 1910s on, many noteworthy black physicians, dentists, and lawyers, such as Drs. C. A. Terrell and L. G. Patterson, had their offices on the second floor. The walk-up was also one of the locations of two of the most important black businesses in Memphis: The Hooks Brothers Photography Studio and the *Memphis World*, a weekly newspaper.

19. MORRIS LIPPMAN BUILDING
(King's Palace Café)
1870s-facade redone in 1919
166 Beale

Although a stone plate indicates the construction of the building to be in 1919, the facade actually was altered that year to celebrate the opening of Morris Lippman's pawn shop. Lippman bought the building in 1908 and the one next door (162/164 Beale) in 1911. He operated his business until 1935 when it became part of Epstein's Loan Office (building #18).

Left to right: The Morris Lippman Building (166 Beale), Commercial Loan Office (168 Beale), Beale Avenue Sales Store (170-172 Beale), ca. 1949.

20. MORRIS PINSTEIN, women's furnishings
(This Is It!)
ca. 1900
167-169 Beale

Morris Pinstein, women's furnishings, early 1970s. Safferstone's Pawn Shop was the last occupant of the building.

Although the facade of this building pales in comparison to Schwab's, it still has great appeal in the arches covering the windows. Max Rossett ran a dry goods store at this address from around 1900 to 1914. The Memphis Tailoring Company occupied 167 Beale from 1916 until the mid-1920s.

Morris Pinstein operated his women's shop and then dry goods store from 1929 to the end of the 1960s. Pinstein liked the location. Before moving in, he ran a business in the Gallina Building (building #24) for eighteen years.

The second floor had several professional offices, notably Dr. A. N. Kittrelle's medical clinic, from 1917 to 1952 (also see building #36). The *Mid-South Liberator*, a weekly black newspaper managed by George J. Strong, was a tenant briefly in 1930. It moved to Hernando, just off of Beale, and lasted about a year longer.

21. COMMERCIAL LOAN OFFICE
(Beale Street Tap Room)
1870s
168 Beale

This building (see photo for building #19) has an interesting facade highlighted by arched window tops and showing a cast-iron storefront. Just before the Yellow Fever Epidemic of 1878, Stephen Clement opened a fish and game depot at this location. "Game depot" referred to businesses which sold fresh fish, game, poultry, and/or oysters; sometimes fruits and meats.

Clement's business was continued in 1884 by Augustus and Michael Fell. Augustus started out as a bell boy at the Overton Hotel but in the late 1870s he became a huckster and poultry dealer at the Beale Street Markethouse (building #28). His brother joined him before they shifted their enterprise to this location. A chicken pen which stood at the rear of the building was a source of fresh poultry for their customers. This 22 by 30 foot structure was as big as some of the low-end dwellings in the area. It must have added considerably to the aromatic ambience of Beale.

Chickens gave way to sharks with the arrival of Nathan Ostrich's Golden Eagle Loan Office in 1900. In 1906 pawnbroker Nathan Karnowsky purchased the building for his business. From 1923 until the early 1960s, it became Isadore Angel's Commercial Loan Office, later operated by Harry S. Davidson who also bought the building.

On the second floor, for over fifty years beginning in 1901, were several African-American physicians and dentists, including E. C. Craigen, W. H. Luster, B. F. McCleave, A. R. Williams, and A. L. Nicholson. One of them, Dr. Fannie M. Kneeland, was the only black female physician in the city during the first decade of this century.

From 1903 to 1905 the black-owned Striker Printing Company, managed by Alonzo L. Hall, occupied the upper floor. In 1908 Hall traded his press for a stethoscope to become a physician. During the same year, William H. Hutton tried to make his weekly newspaper, the *Sentinel*, a success but it failed to see 1909. Previously, he also missed with another weekly, the *Conservator*. At the time, two other African-American papers were more prosperous: the *Bluff City News* at 431 Beale and the *Semi-Weekly Progress* which had various locations. The former was edited by King I. Chambers who churned out his paper until 1919. James E. Washington was a cub reporter for Chambers before becoming editor of the *Progress*, later known as *Our Mail* and the *Western World Reporter*. These papers, among several others, were the forerunners of the longer-lived *Memphis World* and the present-day *Tri-State Defender*.

Ads for two Memphis Banks owned and operated by African-Americans, 1910.

22. BEALE AVENUE SALES STORE, men's clothing
(Strange Cargo)
ca. 1903
170-172 Beale

Around 1903 this building (see photo for building #19) was constructed over the Bayou Gayoso which, if seen from above, resembled a watery serpent slithering across Beale and throughout the district. Before the construction of a sanitary sewer system in 1880, the city used the Bayou as its principal drainage channel: the equivalent of an open cesspool. Many had associated it with the yellow fever epidemics of the 1870s.

Originally, a centrally located stairway to the second floor separated 170 and 172 Beale; and the display windows stood out from each store front, flanking a recessed door. The eave at the upper portion of the building simulates a shallow stone awning.

The first occupants of the building were Benjamin Moyer and Gustave Hecht, who operated a phonograph parlor at 170 Beale; and the Bluff City Commission Company, a stocks, bonds, and securities firm at 172 Beale. This latter address contained mostly pawnshops, such as that of Louis Brod. The Rosenblum Family ran a tailor/clothing business at 170 Beale from around 1909 to 1932. In fact, since 1910, most of the businesses at this street number were clothiers. In 1944 a men's clothing business, Abe Berg's Beale Avenue Sales Store, opened at 170 Beale and eventually took over the entire building.

23. HARWOOD GROCERY COMPANY
(Silky O'Sullivan's Goat Farm)
ca. 1914
171-173 Beale

Around 1914 the last open portion of the Bayou Gayoso, which crossed Beale at this site, was covered over by a two-story building that also consumed a smaller structure next door. It stands out from other buildings with its unique white terra-cotta facade but must now employ a walker made of green steel girders to remain upright. Together, they enclose Beale's controversial attempt at animal husbandry.

William H. Harwood was the first tenant and owned a grocery store at 171 Beale and a wholesale wine and liquor business (the Mohawk Supply Company) at 173 Beale, apparently on the second floor. In 1918 he dropped the liquor distributorship and continued his grocery until 1932. From 1939 into the late 1950s, the Beale Avenue Department Store occupied 171 Beale.

The Harwood Grocery Company, early 1970s. Roy's was the last tenant.

The Rosary Hotel, owned by Jesse Swantsey, was on the second floor from the late 1930s until 1950 when the name, and ownership, changed to the Bluff City Hotel. Swantsey moved his establishment to the second floor of the Gallina Building (building #24). The Rosary had an annex around the corner on S. Third Street from around 1944 until the mid-1960s.

24. GALLINA BUILDING
(Silky O'Sullivan's Patio)
J. C. Alsup, architect
1891
177-181 Beale

Squire Charles Gallina opened a saloon in a one-story building on this site in the late 1860s. After acquiring adjacent property, he commissioned J. C. Alsup to build the Gallina Building in 1891. Better known as Gallina's Exchange, the building housed a saloon, restaurant, and a twenty-room hotel. Performers from the Grand Opera House (building #2) and the Bijou Theater, on the corner of South Main and Linden, used it as a resi-

The Gallina Building, "The Pride of Beale Street," early 1970s.

dence. The Gallina family occupied an apartment on the top floor. Several offices, as well as a gambling and a race horse room, were located upstairs. Gallina owned several horses and his building buzzed with the jabber of the sporting crowd. As an officer of the County Court and as a magistrate, Gallina held court on the second floor over his saloon. He died in 1914.

Over the years other businesses occupied the first floor, including the American Pharmacy, the Morris Pinstein Clothing Store, the Memphis Meat Company, and various dry goods and hardware businesses. Dr. R. Q. Venson, a well-known black dentist, had his office on the second floor for more than twenty-five years, beginning in the early 1940s.

In the 1880s Edgar S. Goens, a popular black barber who also owned quite a bit of property, occupied a building next to Gallina's saloon prior to the construction of the Gallina Building. He continued his business in a new small one-story building next to Gallina's Exchange until his retirement in 1916.

Unfortunately, the facade of this building, supported by six indifferent green-colored steel girders, is all that remains of a glorious past. Each of the hotel rooms had a stone-mantled fireplace; the saloon was lined with walnut paneling; and there were skylights over the stairwells. The incredible facade with its exquisite brickwork, massive brick arches framing the third story windows, and an orange terra-cotta cornice at the top on both sides of the structure, demonstrate why the building was referred to as "The Pride of Beale Street."

Ad for Gallina's Exchange (current #: 177-181 Beale), 1899.

25. LIPPMAN'S/NATHAN'S LOAN OFFICE
(Mr. Handy's Blues Hall/Rum Boogie Café)
1860s
174/176-178 Beale

The addresses cover three separate buildings, although 176-178 Beale look like the same structure. Originally, 178 Beale was smaller in height

Lippman's and Nathan's Loan Office (with black tile), early 1970s.

and length from 174-176 Beale, but sometime after 1888 a new building was constructed to blend in with the other two. In the 1930s the store fronts were remodeled with a tile covering to enclose vent windows just above the entrances. Nathan's has the black tile. The upper portion of the buildings are beautifully done. Note the circular vents, the curved brick overhangs at the window heads which are set in relief from the facade, and the decorative brick work at the cornice near the apex.

From around 1900 to 1916, the Lippman Family ran a pawn shop at 174 Beale. Louis Lerner, the name imprinted on the entranceway tile, bought the business in 1917 and operated it as Lippman's Loan Office through the 1960s. He specialized in diamonds, watches, jewelry, and clothing. A variety of businesses occupied 176-178 Beale: grocers, book dealers, a liquor distributor, the Dixie Photography Studio, and, from the mid-1940s through the 1960s, Nathan's Loan Office.

26. BENSIECK BUILDING
(Rum Boogie Café)
ca. 1921
182-184 Beale

Frank Bensieck owned property on the street, including 182-184 Beale which he purchased in 1880. He operated his bakery and steam ice cream

Left to right: Nathan's Loans (176-178 Beale), the Bensieck Building (182-184 Beale), ca. 1951.

manufacturing business, originally named Berton's Confectionery, at this address from 1878-1902, when he sold it to William C. Smith. Like many small businessmen of the time, he lived on the premise. The original lot contained a three-story elongated structure with ovens in the rear for baking. The present building was built after Bensieck retired.

In 1927 the west side of the building (182 Beale) contained the Beale Street Music Shop before the Blue Light Photography Studio replaced it in 1932. In 1941 Blue Light relocated their facility next to Lansky Brothers (building #4). Howard's Drug Store occupied the east side of the property (184 Beale) from 1921 until 1945.

Paul's Tailoring Shop, operated by Paul J. Vescova, opened around 1948 and remained there throughout the 1960s. He eventually took over the entire building. With his motto, "Where the Smart Crowd Follows," and advertising expert tailoring and the latest in drape styles, Vescova attracted many entertainers, such as Dwight "Gatemouth" Moore. He also had a tie-in with the Palace Theater (see building #35), sponsoring events and acting as a ticket outlet.

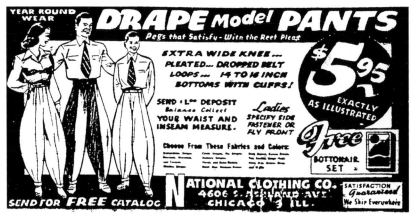

Ad for Drape Model Pants, 1943.

27. MUTUAL FURNITURE CO.
(Silky O'Sullivan's)
ca. 1908
183 Beale

Originally, a one-story building stood on this site. The new two-story structure, built around 1908, had a warehouse behind it, long since removed. The main building contained, at various times, the W. R. Roberts Hardware Company (1909-1913), the Mutual Furniture Company (1915-1928), the Pantaze Drug Store Wholesale House (1929-1946), and the Golden Rule 5 cents and 10 cents to $1 Store (1947-1959).

The name "Mutual Furniture" can still be seen just below the attic vents. To the left and right of the single entrance were large display windows capped by five large vent windows.

Mutual Furniture, with white facade, 1930s. Actually, the photo shows the Pantaze Drug Store Wholesale House, after Mutual Furniture moved out.

Ad for Tuff Green's Orchestra, 1952. The Hippodrome Ballroom was near the Pettit Mansion (building #53) on the northside of Beale.

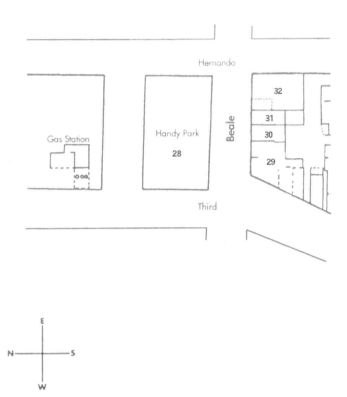

Hernando

Gas Station

Handy Park

28

Beale

32

31

30

29

Third

E

N———+———S

W

Third Street to Hernando

SECTION 3
THIRD STREET TO HERNANDO (RUFUS THOMAS BLVD)

28. BEALE STREET MARKETHOUSE AND COLD STORAGE PLANT
(Handy Park)
Weathers and Weathers, architects
1898
north side of Beale between Third and Hernando (Rufus Thomas Blvd)

Beale Street Market and Cold Storage Plant, 1899. The left part of the building faces Beale.

The markethouse, at the time one of two such facilities in the city, replaced an older, outdated market place built in 1859. It had a centrally located dome flanked by two three-story wings. The first floor contained more than thirty meat, fish, and vegetable stalls, plus such businesses as barber, shoemaker, hat, and tailor shops. The west side of the second and third floors had large cold storage rooms for meat and fish. The east side had space for more stalls. The second floor administrative offices faced Beale and opened onto a large balcony by means of four French doors. The diverse ethnic make-up of the markethouse included a large number of black businesses.

Jug Band, 1939. Similar groups played in Handy Park and on street corners.

In 1930 the markethouse was torn down to make way for Handy Park. It was formally dedicated to the famous composer in 1931. Many blues musicians, such as Robert Johnson, Furry Lewis, and B. B. King, as well as the ever-popular jug bands, played for handouts in the park. After W. C. Handy died in 1958, a statue of him was erected in 1960.

29. BEALE AVENUE MARKET/HANDY SQUARE BUILDING
(Alfred's)
late 1860s
197 Beale

The present building is a combination of 197 and 199/201 Beale. The first address is easy to spot with its white stucco exterior and its set of arched windows lining the front and side of the first floor. A patio, added in 1997, now blocks the view of these windows.

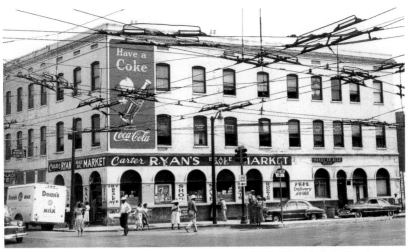

Beale Avenue Market/Handy Square Building, ca. 1950. Note the overhead electric streetcar wires.

From around 1875 to 1914, Louis Vaccaro operated his saloon and restaurant at 197 Beale, specializing in chili and macaroni dishes. He had been on Beale since the mid-1860s, intially as a grocer. With its solid mahogany bar and plate glass mirrors, Vaccaro's saloon was considered to be one of the finest in the area. For around five years, beginning in 1916, the second floor was home to the Memphis Italian Association.

L. VACCARO'S 🌿
.....SALOON AND LUNCH COUNTER,

Chile and Macaroni a Specialty.   COR. BEALE ST. AND HADDEN AVE.

Ad for Louis Vaccaro's Saloon (197 Beale), 1899.

This building was the site of a major Beale Street disaster: the failure of the black-owned Solvent and Fraternal Bank and Trust Company. In 1925 the Solvent Savings Bank and Trust Company moved to 197 from 386 Beale. Shortly after a merger with the Fraternal Savings Bank and Trust Company in October, the bank collapsed on 29 December 1927 with shortages approaching $500,000. The bank failure dealt a severe blow to the Beale Street economy, affecting more than fifteen thousand African-American depositors and over fifty black businesses. Charges were made of embezzlement and mismanagement.

In 1929 the Beale Avenue Market, under various owners, occupied the ground floor for over twenty-five years, until the Forty Minute Cleaning Company replaced it. Since the mid-1920s, the second and third floors, referred to as the "Handy Square Building," contained the offices of several black professionals, such as Dr. O. B. Braithwaite, a dentist, and A. A. Latting, a lawyer.

Next door, at 199/201 Beale, various businesses were present until 1945, when the original King's Palace Café became the last tenant before urban renewal. Earlier, Mrs. Rosa Cohen and her son Solomon ran a dry goods business here from 1900 until 1929.

30. HENRY JOHNSON, barber shop
(WEGR, Fm 103 radio/Performa)
1880s
203 Beale

This building has been totally revamped with a breezeway to the rear. Its facade approximates the original in having two stories and four attic vents. But now the faceless windows resemble minature balconies and the stone window heads look like false eyelashes.

In 1908 there were twelve black-owned barber shops within a four block stretch of Beale which employed 39 barbers. Barbers, such as Edgar S. Goens (see building #24) and Joe Clouston (see building #44), became quite wealthy. Others, like A. P. Martin (see building #45) and Henry Johnson never attained such status but they were competent businessmen. Johnson started out in 1907 in the Beale Street Markethouse. In the photo for building #28, his shop was in the right part of the section under the awning. In 1918 he moved to 203 Beale where he remained until 1929.

Most of the other occupants seemed to come and go like new TV sitcoms. They included men's and women's furnishings, fruits, groceries, and dry goods stores. Still others were jewelers, tailors, watchmakers, and clothes pressers. Harry R. Goldstein's clothing store was here from around 1899 to 1908 and the Dunbar Shoe Store from 1940 to 1945. William B. Tate's C & D Catering had the honor of being the final tenant prior to urban renewal.

31. OAKEY'S SALOON
(Dyer's-Famous Burgers Since 1912)
1884
205 Beale

Oakey's Saloon, upper portion, early 1970s.

This beautiful Victorian-style building was built by John Oakey who had previously occupied the building just to the west of it. The windows are interconnected by brick arches at their heads, on top of which is an attractive cornice that resembles a miniature roof.

Oakey's liquor business dated back to the late 1860s and thrived at this location from 1885 until 1912. He distributed the finest in bourbon and rye whiskies, as well as cigars and tobacco, and also operated a saloon on the premise. Other occupants were the Ridolfi Pharmacy (1913-1915), the White Rose Café (1916-1922), and from the early 1940s through the 1960s, Harry Leviton's Department Store.

32. PANTAZE DRUG STORE NO. 2
(Center for Southern Folklore)
ca. 1884
209-211 Beale

With its windows recessed slightly from the facade to simulate the appearance of columns, this building used to have a cornice at the top. Its window heads are cast-iron. From 1896 through the 1960s, it was a drug store, first that of George H. Battier, then beginning in 1929, the Pantaze Drug Store No. 2. Abe Plough, who founded Plough Pharmaceuticals in 1908, became the proprietor of Battier's Pharmacy around 1914. In 1920 he marketed the popular brand name St. Joseph's Aspirin. Battier's and the Pantaze remained open 24 hours to accommodate the community. They also acted as an emergency room for victims of Beale Street violence.

Pantaze Drug Store, sideview on Hernando (Rufus Thomas Blvd.), ca. 1961. Note the sign for Club Handy.

Around the corner at 195 Hernando was the entrance to the second and third floors. For years it had been used as a rooming house until the late 1930s, when it became the Colored Citizens Association. In the mid-1940s, Andrew "Sunbeam" Mitchell opened a hotel on the third floor and used the second floor as a lounge.

Mitchell helped entertainers, like Little Richard and Roy Brown, who were stranded in Memphis from lack of work. Musicians stayed in the hotel and were charged a nominal fee for a bowl of chili, a feast fondly remembered by Beale Street regulars. The second floor lounge began as a place for jam sessions where local and out-of-town musicians played. At one time it was called the Domino Lounge and after W. C. Handy died, renamed the Club Handy. Jazz and blues performers, such as Lionel Hampton, Dizzy Gillespie, Sonny Boy Williamson, and Little Walter, among many others, performed there. Bill Harvey, the guru of Memphis musicians, led the house band in the late 1940s. B. B. King eventually took over the band. B. B. had played in Mitchell's Lounge beginning in the early 1950s.

CLUB HANDY
Presents

B. B. KING
AND HIS ORCHESTRA

Monday Night, November 26, 1962
9 until

$2.00

Advance

At Door

$2.50

BOBBY BLAND & AL BRAGGS

AT

THE CLUB HANDY

Sunday Night, July 16, 1961
From 9 'Till

ADMISSION - Advance $2.00   At Door $2.50

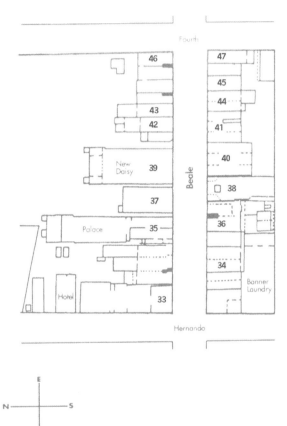

Hernando to Fourth Street

SECTION 4
HERNANDO TO FOURTH STREET

33. A. GREENER AND SONS, dry goods
(future site of Pat O' Brien's - original building demolished)
1923
308-312 Beale

Greener's Department Store, 1940s.

The original three-story building, which stood on the northeast corner of Beale and Hernando (Rufus Thomas Blvd.), was occupied by grocers from 1869 to 1918. Frank McLaughlin, who had been a partner in his brother John's grocery since the early 1870s, was in business at this address from around 1877 until 1910. In 1923 the building was demolished and a new one built for the black-owned Fraternal Savings Bank and Trust Company at a cost of $40,000.

On 7 January 1924, the bank opened for business at this, their new location. It merged with the Solvent Savings Bank on 1 October 1927 (see building #29). During this period, the second and third floor tenants consisted of four African-American businesses: the Memphis General Brokerage Company, and the Universal, North Carolina Mutual, and National Benefit Life Insurance Companies.

Greener's Department Store served the community from 1928 until the early 1960s, when it became the Harris Department Store. Both were mirror images of Schwab's.

34. P. WEE'S SALOON
(Hard Rock Café - original building demolished)
ca. 1890
317 Beale

The most famous saloon on Beale was P. Wee's, named after Virgilio

P. Wee's Saloon, 1947. An earlier view of P. Wee's may be seen in the cover photograph.

Maffei, an Italian immigrant who arrived in Memphis during the mid-1870s. He started out as a bartender at Gallina's Exchange but opened his own saloon in 1884 a few doors away from its final location at 317 Beale. Maffei, only four-and-a-half-feet tall, was supposedly so strong that he beat boxer Jack Johnson, and others, in arm wrestling. During hot summer evenings, he swam from the foot of Beale across the Mississippi River to the Arkansas side.

Maffei liked to gamble and played with some of the biggest gamesters east of the Mississippi River. Local high rollers, like Mac Harris and Casino Henry, frequented P. Wee's. Dressed in a chesterfield coat, pin-striped trousers, patent leather shoes, a homburg hat, and with his mustache twisted up at the ends, Harris looked like a stately gentleman. In contrast Casino Henry appeared nervous, constantly chewed gum, and had a strange habit of walking down the middle of Beale Street.

A cigar stand, with a painting of Othello and Desdemona hanging above it, stood just inside the saloon's door. Other than the bar, there were billiard

W. C. Handy, Father of the Blues, Carnegie Hall, 1938.

and pool tables and an area for dice and card games in the rear. A policy (or numbers) game operated from the second floor.

Many of the saloons and cafés on Beale had some form of gambling. To protect themselves from periodic raids, the clubs had an early warning system. P. Wee's used a lookout man with a buzzer hidden under his shirt, as well as a backup unit that played dominoes all day and watched for suspicious characters. The police had a way of overcoming these obstacles. During one incident, an undercover cop was first sent in. When the regular police arrived, the undercover man grabbed the lookout's hand to keep him from pressing the buzzer. The police took the entire back room to jail but they were only fined one dollar each.

Maffei decided to take it easy and during the 1890s made Lorenzo and Angelo Pacini partners. Around 1913 he returned to Italy. The Pacini brothers operated the saloon until approximately 1920. Sam, Lorenzo's son, kept it in the family until his death in 1941.

In the early 1900s, P. Wee's was a musician's hangout with a backroom closet crammed with instruments. At the time, the saloon had the city's only pay phone over which prospective clients contacted band leaders, especially W. C. Handy. He acted as agent for a number of different bands selected from the pool of musicians at P. Wee's. In 1909, according to legend, Handy wrote "Mister Crump," later named "Memphis Blues," on the saloon's cigar counter. Handy's band performed "Mister Crump" at Edward H. Crump's mayoralty campaign. Out of friendship, Handy dedicated "St. Louis Blues" to the Pacini Brothers.

In later years P. Wee's became a pool hall and then a laundry. In 1956 a one-story building replaced the original structure which, in turn, fell to the wrecking ball in the early 1970s. A new building was constructed in the 1980s.

The original location of P. Wee's was several doors east of the entrance to the Hard Rock Café which subsumes the old street numbers 311,

313, 315, 317, and 319 Beale. A three-story nineteenth-century building, which may be seen at the far right in the cover photo, once stood where the main part of the café is now located. At the time (1915), the upper floors contained the Lincoln Hotel.

In the cover photo, a sign labeled "Café" marks the entranceway to the New Orleans Café (313 Beale). Initially owned by J. G. Paris and later by Peter and Louis Liberakis, the restaurant was in business from around 1914 to 1935. Advertising respectability, service, quality, and cleanliness, the restaurant was narrow and long with a white bathroom-like tile floor. Three fans with pull strings and two large globed light fixtures dangled from its tin ceiling. On the left, toward the rear, was a soda fountain with ten white ice cream stools. The right side contained tables and chairs set against a slated wood wall. Mirrors, framed in wood, hung on the wall above which were coat hooks. At the front was a display case stuffed with cigar boxes and a check-out counter which held two candy machines, one for peanuts and the other for gum balls. Behind the counter were glass cases containing stacks of canned goods on top of which were two chaulk boards that listed the daily menu.

35. PALACE THEATER
(The Legends Patio-original building demolished)
1919
324 Beale

The original three-story building at this location, probably built in the 1870s, contained over the years a variety of businesses. Around 1910 Sam Zerilla remodeled one part of the building for his Pastime Theater which was one of the first movie houses for blacks in Memphis. Zerilla, an Italian immigrant, had been a clarinetist with John Philip Sousa's band.

In 1919, about two years after the Pastime closed, Anselmo Barrasso and the Pacini brothers, Lorenzo and Angelo, built the Palace Theater which became the entertainment showcase for blacks in the Mid-South. They retained the original building as a lobby, using the upper floors for offices, and added an extension to the rear which contained the main part of the theater. The photo shows the original facade which underwent a major renovation in 1949. At a cost of $60,000, the third floor was removed, a new glass front and marquee installed, and the lobby was modernized. The Palace was torn down in 1972.

The Palace was the only local member of the Theater Owners and Bookers Association (T.O.B.A.), a circuit of theaters which catered to black audiences. The theaters were located in an area roughly bounded by New

York, Dallas, Chicago, and Pittsburgh. In the 1920s touring shows, such as Bessie Smith's *Steamboat Days* and Ma Rainey's *Paramount Flappers*, criss-crossed the country on the T.O.B.A. circuit. Along with vaudeville skits, these shows included blues singers, even opera singers, dancers, acrobats, jugglers, comics, chorus girls, and an orchestra. The cream of black enter-tainment played the Palace, including Ethel Waters, the Mills Brothers,

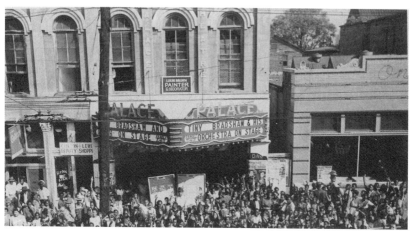

Left to right: The Palace Theater (324 Beale), the One Minute Dairy Lunch (326-328 Beale), 1947.

Butterbeans and Susie, Mamie Smith, Blanche Calloway, and Lil Green.

The Palace also showed films and had talent contests. Amateur night originated in the twenties but its heyday was from the 1930s through the 1950s. It took place on Tuesdays (later, on Wednesdays), and may have included anything from singers to tire-blowing competitions. In the mid-1930s, Nat D. Williams, a teacher and historian, and Rufus Thomas, a young Memphis entertainer, hosted amateur night. Williams, the master of cer-emonies, acted as the straight man to Thomas' tomfoolery. In the early 1940s, Rufus took over Williams' role, while Robert "Bones" Couch became the clown. Couch dressed himself in baggy pants, big enough to fit three men, a funny tie and hat, and a long coat which nearly reached the floor on his small four-foot eleven-inch frame.

Winners were selected by the volume of audience approval and re-ceived either cash, groceries, or a combination of groceries and cash prizes. Later, anyone who appeared on stage received one dollar. Limp performances were suffocated by an outpouring of boos, catcalls, and the stomping of feet. In the 1930s, Angelo Pacini, in his role as the "Lord High Executioner," added the finishing touch by shooting the act with his pearl-handled re-volver loaded with blanks. "Bones" had a different method. To escort the

Ad for the Brown Skin Models, Palace Theater, 1942. The Brown Skin Models, managed by Irwin C. Miller, was a vaudeville show consisting of thirty-five entertainers. Its home base was New York City, although several chorus girls and musicians were from Memphis.

act off, he may have swung onto the stage by means of a rope, screaming like Tarzan, or come out with a long hook, or beating on a parade drum. Some of the winners became big stars, like B. B. King, Bobby "Blue" Bland, Al Hibbler, Johnny Ace, Roscoe Gordon, Isaac Hayes, and Rufus Thomas.

A Midnight Ramble took place on Thursday nights for white audiences. Sometimes the attraction was a name jazz orchestra, such as Duke Ellington or Count Basie. At other times, touring road shows, like the Brown Skin Models, put on entertainment strictly for adults which featured off-color jokes and scantily-clad chorus girls.

Ad for Charles Booker's Select Orchestra, 1922. Booker was a composer and recording artist who later moved to New York.

Ad for Curtis Johnson's Jazz Band, 1921.

36. GEORGE R. JACKSON, drug store
(People's Billiard Club - original building demolished)
ca. 1901
323-327 Beale

For several decades before 1900, the region between 323 and 337 Beale remained, for the most part, an open field. A two-story brick structure at this site was the first building to fill out the space. The current new building recaptures the flavor and feel of the original.

In 1893 George R. Jackson opened his New Era Pharmacy at 205 Beale (building #31). It was the first African-American-owned drug store in Memphis. Flossie, his sister and also a pharmacist, worked with him. The store was moved to the east side of this building (327 Beale) in 1901. One can only theorize that his relocation east of Fourth Street in 1911 from 327 Beale was due to the murder of prominent businessman Milton L. Clay in front of his store (see building #47). In 1933 Jackson left Beale to open a pharmacy on Mississippi Boulevard. His sister continued to operate the store after his death in 1935.

People's Billiard Parlor is the most recent of a long line of pool halls at 327 Beale. They included the Rex Pool Room and, in 1933, the Stagg Billiard Parlor owned by Elmer Atkinson. Atkinson also ran Elmer's Luncheonette at the same address. He closed in 1944 but was succeeded by John Brown's billiard and restaurant business in 1949.

Photographer Ernest Withers was at 327 Beale from around 1964 to 1971. After serving in the all-black Memphis police unit during the 1940s, he became well-known for his photos of the Civil Rights Movement and local African-American life. Around 1995 he returned to the street at 333 Beale (building #40).

The west side of the building (323 Beale) contained Morris Rosenthal's dry goods store from 1902 to 1934, followed by Mattie Bryant's beauty and barber shop and Ernest C. Outten's watch repair business. Both were in operation until the 1950s. The final occupant, James Wyatt's hat shop, had been on Beale for over fifty years.

On the second floor, beginning in 1901, were the offices of Drs. J. C. Hairston, A. N. Kittrelle, and J. C. Clark, a dentist. Dr. Hairston was one of the most distinguished physicians in Memphis. Realizing that the city lacked good hospital facilities for African-Americans, Hairston opened a ten-bed unit in his home. In 1917 he and Clark moved to 149 Beale (building #10) and Kittrell to 169 Beale (building #20).

Dr. L. R. Ross and other professionals took over the floor. With his slogan, "My Tooth Doctor," Ross outfitted his office with state of the art dental equipment and attracted crowds of customers with his courteous and efficient service. During the 1920s, he advertised gold crowns and bridges at the special price of four dollars each, while a full set of teeth cost fifteen dollars. Teeth were pulled free with other dental work. Ross remained at this address until 1942.

37. ONE MINUTE DAIRY LUNCH
(Willie Mitchell's Legends)
1941
326-328 Beale

This building, probably built by Paul Zerilla and Joe Maceri at the same time as the New Daisy Theater (see photo for building #35), took the place of an older two-story building constructed in the 1880s. Its occupants were mostly grocers, barbers, and restaurant and saloon proprietors, until 1921, when the One Minute moved in. The restaurant remained open until 1953.

The One Minute, a popular rendezvous, specialized in footlong hot dogs, chili dogs, and root beer. Owned by "Hot Dog Jimmy" Bikas, in the 1930s the Café sold 3600 hot dogs per day. Andrew Chaplin, the drummer with "Hulbert's Lo-Down Houns" in 1930, begged the leader to change the name of the band because he got tired of being ribbed every time he bought a hot dog in the One Minute. In the late 1950s, Jeff's "On Beale" Hot Pit Bar-B-Q opened. Some claimed it sold the best in town.

38. DAISY THEATER
(Daisy Music Interpretive Center)
1917
329-331 Beale

Daisy Theater, early 1970s.

In 1917, about a year after Sam Zerilla closed the Pastime Theater (see building #35), he built the Daisy Theater, another movie house. In 1929 it premiered the short, *St. Louis Blues*, which starred the great blues singer Bessie Smith. Smith, dressed in fancy furs, drove up in a limousine with W. C. Handy. In a scene more reminiscent of Hollywood, they stepped from their car onto a red carpet which took them past an enthusiastic crowd into the theater. During the 1930s and 1940s, a popular feature at the Daisy was Money Night. Held every Wednesday evening at 9:00 P.M., the pot was increased each week until someone won.

The facade is Moorish in character with a ribbed interior dome which stretches upward toward a one-half circle of lights. Originally, each side of the building contained small stores, one a candy shop and the other a shoe shine parlor. The interior still has the original balcony and wall embellishments. Patrons entered the theater on either side of the stage which faced the rear.

39. NEW DAISY THEATER
1941
330 Beale

New Daisy Theater, 1941.

Paul Zerilla and Joe Maceri built the New Daisy to replace two other theaters at this location. The reasoning behind trading one for two is not clear, since the older theaters taken together were much larger and only twenty to thirty years old. In the trade-off, the One Minute Dairy Lunch (building #37) next door got a new building, while a much smaller structure was built to partially fill in the alleyway to the east of the theater (see photo for building #42). This latter building, initially occupied by Kane's Big Dipper Ice Cream Store, became the Harlem House in 1950, a restaurant chain which had outlets all over the downtown area.

The New Daisy showed films and occasionally had live music. Its architecture has an art deco flair, highlighted by a lattice pattern of brick work and elongated vents above the marquee.

40. EDWARD BUFFINGTON, tailor shop
(Down Home Iceworks and Food Factory/Y Not Souvenirs/
EEL Etc. - original building demolished)
ca. 1912
333-335-337 Beale

Right to left: Buffington Tailors (333-335-337 Beale); Moses Franklin, meat market (339-341-343 Beale); the Rudner Building (345 Beale); A. P. Martin, barber shop (347 Beale), 1942. Photo taken from under the New Daisy marquee.

In the mid-1890s a couple of small homes, a saw shop, and a horse shed which stood here were torn down. An attractive one-story building was finally erected in 1912. It had an upper facade of white tile with dark trim and a centrally located ornamentation which resembled a clock. A portion of the building may be seen in the photo. In the 1960s a slab of unsightly aluminum siding - an attempt at remodeling - was placed over the upper portion, in effect destroying the character and charm of the original facade. The building was demolished in the 1980s.

Edward Buffington began his tailoring business in Greenwood, Mississippi, in 1902. He relocated to Memphis around 1919 and opened at 356 Beale on the northeast corner of Beale and Fourth. His move to 337 Beale, replacing Edward J. Gabriel's billiard parlor, came in 1928. Although he died in 1951, the store remained open until the early 1970s. Buffington's business became one of the largest in the South, specializing in clothes for the connoisseur, and eventually employed nine expert tailors. The company had sales representatives covering the entire South, as well as a branch in Chicago.

The other part of the building, 333 and 335 Beale, had a succession of restaurants: the Peter Swift Cafeteria, the Elite Café, the Sugar Boll Restaurant, Willie's Café, and Gus Marestes' Café. The longest running was the New York Café (333 Beale) owned by Daniel and Jerry Touliatos from 1914 to 1925. Thomas Pappas ran the New York Confectionary Company at 335 Beale from 1934 to 1944. He also owned Joe's Lunch Room (building #4).

Robert Henry, for years an important booking agent and club owner on Beale, ran a record store and then a pool room, first at 343 (see building #41) and then at 335 Beale. Henry's pool room was the final business at this location before urban renewal.

41. MOSES FRANKLIN, meat market (Alleyway to Beale St. Tatoos & Ernest C. Withers, photographer/Pizza On Beale - original building demolished) late 1860s 339-341-343 Beale

This appealing two-story brick building was conceived in three equal sections, each of them having four elongated windows perched above a set of window vents and an entranceway (see photo for building #40). At the top was an eave, probably covered in tile, which may have been added after construction. The building was vacated in 1964 and eventually torn down in the mid-1970s.

Butcher Moses Franklin, from 1902 until his death in 1916, ran a meat store at this location. Other occupants included tailors, grocers, retaurateurs, clothiers, and barbers, among others. One of the barbers, Elias Stinson, was in business from 1937 to 1963. There was also a tire business (the Fulton Vulcanizing Tire Company, 1921-1923), two drug firms (one named the Indian Herb Medicine Company, 1911-1913), and two music stores (The Beale Street Music Shop, 1921-1924, and Robert Henry's Record Exchange, 1944-1950) located here.

In 1919 Madam Gold S. Morgan Young arrived from Greenwood, Mississippi, to open the Gorine Beauty College at 432 Beale, about a block east of this location. She expanded her business to include 341 Beale from 1926 to 1932, when the Chiles and Bridgeforth Beauty Parlor became tenants. The Gorine Beauty College remained open into the 1970s. Mrs. Young not only trained beauticians but manufactured hair dressing and beauty aids. She held several degrees in the field of cosmetology and, during the 1920s, was President of the National Beauty Culturists League.

The headquarters of many professionals were on the second floor, including those of dentist Warren Waters and Dr. W. T. Prater and, in the 1920s and early 1930s, the living quarters and offices of several ministers.

Very briefly, in 1906, the three Gillis Brothers operated a first-class and well-appointed hotel on the second and a grocery store on the ground floor. They also had another grocery outside the Beale area. Although these entrepreneurs were mainly in the grocery business, their most important connection to Beale was the World's Supply Company and Exchange Mart, located at 427 Beale from around 1908 to 1915. They advertised new and used furniture and appliances, repair work, shipping and storage service, and even toiletries and perfumes. They were the sole distributors of My Flower and Ever-Lasting Love-Me Quick, two colognes made of flower extracts.

42. THE MONARCH SALOON
(future home of Dreamland Barbecue)
1870s, facade probably remodeled 1890s
340 Beale

With a facade marked by a multicolored variegated brickwork, a beautiful carved stone window emplacement which recalls the Old World, and a cast-iron store front, this building is one of the most attractive on the street. The original eave at the cornice was removed in the 1950s and later replaced during renovation of the facade. Its beauty belied the fact that the Monarch ranked high as one of the most notorious gambling joints and saloons on Beale. Its heyday was from around 1902 through the teens.

Mirrors, which totally encased the lobby, hung above black cushioned seats that were built into the wall. The entire length of the beautiful mahogany bar had brass rail fittings. The gambling room in back was reinforced by brick and barricaded by a steel door to protect it from raids. Upstairs a dance hall and poker rooms drew all kinds of patrons. W. C. Handy frequented the dance hall to listen to its piano thumpers, Bennie Frenchie and Sonny Butts. Jim Kinnane, owner of the Monarch, also operated sa-

The Monarch Saloon (Billiards), 1941. To the right is the Oriental Café (Chop Suey Café), 342 Beale; to the left, part of the Harlem House Café.

loons in North Memphis. He was a big-time politician, boss of the first ward.

The Monarch, nicknamed the "Castle of Missing Men" because of its reputation for murders, conveniently stood near the undertaking establishment of Levi McCoy. McCoy lay claim to most of those killed in the saloon. The Monarch was home to some of the toughest characters on the street, like Bad Sam, Cousin Hog, and Long Charlie. It also earned some notoriety for a famous duel in 1918 between Ben Griffin, a short but tough hood, and Johnny Margerum, white underworld boss of the Monarch.

Griffin carried two guns, one in his belt and another tucked away in a shoulder holster. Even the police stayed clear of him. One evening, after checking one of his pistols at the door, Griffin went upstairs to gamble. He returned downstairs and went into the kitchen where, for some reason, he got into a fight with another patron. Margerum, just entering the saloon, heard the commotion and rushed to the kitchen. He ordered Griffin to stop hitting the man. Griffin shouted back, "I'm going to hit this man wherever I please," and pulled his second gun firing two bullets into Margerum. As Margerum fell, he fired back. Both men died within ten minutes. Such events became part of the folklore of Beale Street.

THE MONARCH SALOON
THE FINEST COLORED SALOON IN THE WORLD. EVERYTHING UP-TO-DATE
Headquarters for all Hotel Waiters. also
...Wines, Liquors and Cigars...
S. I. McWILLIAMS & JIM WALLACE, MIXOLOGISTS
NEW PHONE 2496
340 BEALE AVE.

Letterhead used on the Monarch Saloon stationary, 1908.

43. ORIENTAL CAFÉ
(original building demolished)
1860s
342 Beale

In the photo for building #42, the Oriental Café resembles Hammitt Ashford's Saloon (building #46) in brick work, window size, and placement of vents, except for a large parapet. A year or two after the photo was taken, the facade was modernized with the elimination of one window and one vent and the covering-over of the brick (see photo for building #46).

From around 1900 to 1910, A. B. Williamson ran a saloon at this location which may have been tied-in with the notorious Monarch Saloon (building #42). In 1907 his business was briefly advertised as "amusements" (i.e., motion pictures). For certain, it was not family fare.

At one point, during the teens, the two buildings were joined. However, in 1919, Lau C. Chu rented 342 Beale, once again separating them. He lived on the second floor and opened up the Oriental Café on the first. Although the name was changed to the Chop Suey Café in 1921 by Moy Ming, the new owner, the restaurant was always known as the "Oriental," probably because the name was set into the entranceway tile floor. An extremely popular and enduring restaurant, it stayed in business, with several ownership changes, into the late 1960s.

44. RUDNER BUILDING
(Pizza On Beale - original building demolished)
ca. 1870
345 Beale

Originally a three-story building, the top floor was removed in 1924 (see photo for building #40). The upper facade shows "1924 Rudner." Jacob Rudner, born in Austria, had been on the street since 1890 with a clothing/ dry goods business, initially at 342 Beale and, until 1925, at 147 Beale (building #9). He soon retired and died in 1936. Rudner was a good businessman and owned several properties on the street, including 157, 171/173, 323/327, and 345 Beale. There were several free blacks in Memphis prior to the Civil War. One of them, Joseph Clouston, Sr., became an important businessman and landowner. Born a slave in 1814, Clouston was a barber, who through good business acummen, bought his freedom. Around 1850 he moved to Memphis and purchased this property. It was the first of fourteen he bought in the 1850s. During the 1860s and 1870s, he operated a combination barber/grocery shop at this address. His son, Joseph, Jr., also a barber by trade, became one of the first African-American city councilmen in 1873. The Cloustons eventually owned property in downtown Memphis and several farms outside the city. The elderly Clouston died in 1894 and his son, in 1898, at the age of 50.

In the 1880s and 1890s, the dominant business was the saloon of John Miller and Edward Cunney. Similarly, from the turn of the century onwards, barber and shaving salons ranked supreme. There were notable exceptions, such as the jewelry shops of Jeff Reed and E. C. Outten and for five years, beginning in 1925, the St. Charles Hotel run by J. L. Gilliland and Mrs. V. A. Bailey. Their ad read: "Neatly furnished rooms $3.00 a week and up, café in connection...."

The longest running occupant was Hugh C. Eggleston whose store sign simply read, "Eggleston the Tailor." Eggleston first opened his shop next door at 343 Beale but moved to 345 Beale in 1933. He remained here until the mid-1970s. Eggleston, who learned his craft working for seven years with Edward Buffington (building #40), was a first-class tailor, making suits for wealthy plantation owners. He died in the mid-1990s.

45. ARTHUR P. MARTIN, barber shop
(west portion of Have a Nice Day Café
- original building demolished)
ca. 1900
347 Beale

In the 1880s a two-story building once stood on this site but it was torn down in the 1890s. Around 1900 a new one-story building was constructed. Its white front, with a facade which resembles a classy White Castle hamburger joint, is seen in the photo for building #40.

In 1906 Arthur P. Martin became a partner in Henry Harris' barber business located on Main Street. After Harris died, Martin moved the shop to 347 Beale in 1915. Following his death in 1955, his widow carried on until the early 1970s. Martin also operated a barber college out of his home at 454 Beale from the late 1920s to the late 1940s. Martin, no relation to the prominent professional family of the same name, founded the Memphis Red Sox in 1919, the first professional African-American baseball team in the city (also see building #16).

The longevity of Martin's business and the smallness of the building precluded a wide variety of occupants. However, Charles Pang had a Chinese laundry at this location from around 1902 to 1910. He was succeeded by Sing Wah who only remained until 1914.

46. HAMMITT ASHFORD'S SALOON
(W. C. Handy's Memphis Home - original building demolished)
1860s
350 Beale

Hammitt Ashford's Saloon (Wilson's Drugs), ca. 1942. Note the Avalon Pool Room a few doors down.

This was the site of Hammitt Ashford's Saloon, reputed to have been the fanciest wateringhole on Beale during the first decade of the 1900s. On the first floor, rows of chairs lined one side of the room, facing a mahogany bar which ran the length of the opposite side. The center of the room contained several marble tables, a perfect location to view the numerous paintings of women which covered the walls. In another section were pool and billiard tables. The upstairs had a glittering carpeted lounge with muslin drapes, white wallpaper, and imported chandeliers.

The saloon was the scene of one of the most tragic events on Beale: the murder of five gamblers by Wild Bill Latura in 1908. Latura, a white businessman who had a penchant for gambling, had a trigger temper and vindictive personality. His killing spree concerned an old grudge with Ashford. Brought to trial, the twenty-four-year-old Latura was found not guilty on the grounds of insanity. He was also never convicted of beating a man to death with a baseball bat nor for killing a man at his brother's saloon. In 1916 Sandy Lyons, a Memphis policeman, outdrew Latura and shot him to death.

Ashford wore snazzy, expensive clothes and a three-carat diamond tiepin. He later left for St. Louis, after having been acquitted for the murder of gambler Fatty Grimes. It may be poetic license that the undertaking establishment of Barnett and Lewis replaced Ashford's saloon in 1910.

The Wilson Drug Company occupied the building from 1941 through the 1960s. It was a popular hangout for high school students, a neighborly place where one could relax and sip an ice cream soda or leave a message for a friend.

Ad for Barnett and Lewis Undertakers, 1915.

47. PANAMA CAFÉ
(future home of Have a Nice Day Café
- original building demolished)
ca. 1897
351 Beale

The original three-story building was torn down in the 1970s and replaced by the present structure. The older building contained a saloon and gambling house which had tragic endings for three of its owners.

Panama Café (on corner), 1940s.

In 1902 Milton L. Clay changed this Italian grocery, operated by Dominico Volpi, into a saloon. He also owned a barber shop next door at 349 Beale. Clay, a black man, graduated from Fisk University and taught school in Mississippi before becoming a Memphis businessman. He became vice-president of the Solvent Savings Bank and Trust Company. Clay's saloon was a favorite of the race horse and betting crowd. Before the state outlawed pari-mutuel betting in 1906, Memphis had legalized horseracing, first at Montgomery Park and later at the North Memphis Driving Park. In 1911 a vindictive customer, who had been beaten up by the police in Clay's saloon, took it out on its owner by murdering him in front of Jackson's Drug store at 327 Beale (building #36).

In 1909 Clay went into the hay and grain business. He let Thomas R. Dockery, his barkeeper, run the saloon (351 Beale) and Charles Givens, his manager, operate the barber shop (349 Beale). Dockery died under suspicious circumstances in an automobile accident in Mississippi around 1914.

Amos "Mack" McCullough succeeded Dockery. At various times McCullough ran several billiard parlors, a grocery store, a restaurant, a cab company, and just before his death, the Union Drug Store. In 1921 he changed the name of his restaurant at 351 Beale to the Panama Café and put in a billiard parlor next door. His cab company operated out of the Café. McCullough advertised his place as "The Panama Soda Fountain Café," where you would find good fellowship, and good food and drink. In actuality his Café and billiard parlor had, like many businesses on Beale, a backroom for gambling and a hidden quantity of bootleg liquor. Jimmy Turpin operated the games which had three shifts and ran all night. McCullough lost $37,000 when the Solvent and Fraternal Bank and Trust Company failed in 1927 (see building #29). In 1929 he was shot three times just as he opened the door to his house, apparently the victim of a gangland slaying.

The Panama Café/Cab Company stayed in operation throughout the 1930s, until it was converted to a liquor store around 1940 and afterward a legitimate restaurant, Selma's Luncheonette.

Sam Stevenson, who had been a taxi driver with the Panama Cab Company, opened the Busy Bee Taxi Company next door at 349 Beale in 1938. A few years later he operated a billiard parlor at the same address. He sold both businesses in the 1950s.

Ad for Pace and Handy Music Company, 1915.

Mamie Smith and Her Jazz Hounds, New York, 1920. Mamie Smith (1883-1946) was the first African-American singer to record a blues. Although "Crazy Blues" was her second record (recorded 10 August 1920), it was the one which attracted the most attention and which opened the market for other blues singers. Over one million copies were sold across the nation in the first seven months of its release. Mamie became a huge star and was paid $1000-$1500 for her stage appearances, a very hefty sum in the early 1920s. She toured the T.O.B.A. circuit with her revue and played the Palace in Memphis several times. At many of her engagements, lines formed around the block. Mamie made several films, including Jail House Blues in 1929.

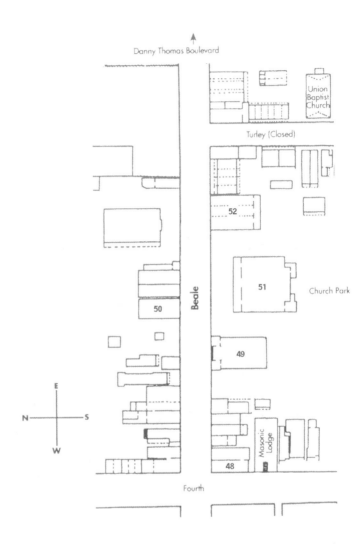

Fourth Street to Turley (This street no longer goes through to Beale)

SECTION 5
FOURTH STREET TO TURLEY
(THIS STREET
NO LONGER GOES THROUGH TO BEALE)

48. MIDWAY CAFÉ
(building demolished)
1870s
357 Beale

Midway Café, late 1960s.

Samuel Volpi operated his grocery store at this location from the 1890s until 1907. Two years later Joseph Raffanti opened a saloon which he named the Midway Café in 1928. Although the type of business changed from a saloon to a billiard parlor, a restaurant, and finally a liquor store, the Raffanti Family remained at the helm. The building was torn down in 1970.

This legendary café was well-known for its blues pianists. During the 1930s, the front part of the building contained a restaurant which served hot plate dishes like spaghetti and meatballs. In the back was a gambling room containing crap tables and next to it a room with a piano.

Memphis Slim's first job took place at the café in June 1931. Booker T. Laury, Piano Red, Roosevelt Sykes, and Sunnyland Slim were a few of the other pianists who played the Midway.

49. FIRST BAPTIST BEALE STREET CHURCH
(Historical First Baptist Beale Church)
Edward C. Jones and Mathias H. Baldwin, architects
1868-1885
379 Beale

The beginning of the First Baptist Beale Street Church must start with the break off of a group of white parishioners from the First Baptist Church

under the leadership of Pastor Peter S. Gayle. In 1849 he organized the South Memphis Baptist Church, later renamed the Beale Baptist Church, which stood about 150 feet west of this location. However, most of the membership were free African-Americans and slaves. This was due, in part, to the interest of Baptists to instruct blacks in religious teachings. But city ordinances barred blacks from preaching to a congregation and also required that a white man be present during services. During the Civil War, after Memphis fell to Union forces in June 1862, such regulations disappeared. Nevertheless, for a few years, the Beale Baptist Church continued under the

First Baptist Beale Street Church, early 1880s.

leadership of Rev. John Bateman, a white pastor.

Around 1863 the church, which had opened its basement as a school for blacks, was burned to the ground by angry citizens. At this point, the white and black membership separated, the former eventually building the Central Baptist Church on Second Street, just north of Beale. Rev. Morris Henderson, with several other African-Americans, held services in the basement of the Second Presbyterian Church on the northeast corner of Beale and Main.

Under Henderson's leadership, this poor and small congregation put a downpayment on the lot where the present church is now located. It was completely paid off in October 1866, mostly from member contributions. The only donation from the white community was $50 made by Confederate General Nathan Bedford Forrest, one-time slave dealer and future Grand Wizard of the KKK. The congregation worshipped in a "brush arbor" before a small shed was built. In 1868 the basement was completed, but due to a lack of funds, the church was not finished until 1885 at a total cost of over $44,000.

The architecture of the church is only a slight reminder of its past beauty. What remains is two towers on either side of a rossette pattern of windows, which resemble the rotary dial of a phone, and three large arched doorways. Originally, as seen in the photo, a great deal of Victorian ornamentation was present in the pediment and in its towers. The right (west) tower supported a celtic cross sitting on top of a cupola-like structure. In the early 1880s, the cross fell into the center of the church during a windstorm. The other tower (east) bore a tin statue of John The Baptist pointing to Heaven. One day a drunk climbed the roof and hacked off one of the arms. The end came in 1938 when lightening struck the statue. Workmen went up to make repairs but accidentally dropped the statue off the roof, bending it beyond repair.

The church published two of the earliest African-American newspapers in the city. The first, in 1884, was the *Memphis Watchman* edited by Rev. J. Lott. A couple of years later, Rev. Taylor Nightingale, pastor of the church, became co-editor with J. T. Turner. Turner, a dealer in staple and fancy groceries, published the newspaper out of his grocery store. In 1888 the *Memphis Free Speech and Headlight* replaced the *Watchman* and was put together at the church.

Ida B. Wells, a teacher at the Clay Street School, became part owner with Rev. Nightingale and in 1890 became the editor. In her articles, Wells criticized the "Jim Crow Laws" and the treatment of African-Americans as second-class citizens. In 1892 a friend of Wells, Tom Moss, was lynched by a posse of 75 masked men. He and thirty others were arrested and jailed after a shootout which left three wounded white men. The incident took place a couple of miles south of Beale. The charges were rape and conspiracy. Moss and two others were taken from the jail by trickery and then brutally murdered in a field in North Memphis. Moss owned the People's Grocery Store which had been competing successfully with another grocery owned by a white man, W. H. Barrett. Most people believed that the accusations were made by Barrett to get rid of the competition. He and others were known to sell illegal liquor and hold crap games. On the day of the murders, a group of whites drew up a letter blaming Barrett for the trouble.

This incident set Wells on a crusade to denounce lynchings. She wrote scathing articles about the poor treatment given blacks in Memphis and recommended that they should leave the city. Within two months of the Tom Moss lynching, 6000 had left. In May 1892, as Wells journeyed to New York, an irate crowd ransacked the offices of the *Free Speech* and destroyed the type and furnishings. Wells never returned to Memphis but continued her anti-lynching crusade from the North and from Europe.

50. TRI-STATE BANK
(Charles E. Carpenter Law Offices)
1907
386 Beale

On 16 December 1946, the Tri-State Bank, still in operation at the corner of Beale and Main, opened in this building. This was the third black-owned bank in the city. The first, the Solvent Savings Bank and Trust Company, started out in a building east of and next to 386 Beale in 1906. In 1914 it moved to 386 and then, in 1925, to 197 Beale on the corner of Beale and Third. Its failure, after a merger in 1927, is discussed under building #29.

On the second floor of 386 Beale were the offices of the Pace and Handy Music Company, one of the first such enterprises in the United States owned by African-Americans. It opened in 1913 and remained there until 1918, when both Harry Pace and W. C. Handy moved to New York.

Tri-State Bank, 1946. The Pace and Handy Music Company was on the second floor.

51. CHURCH'S PARK AND AUDITORIUM
(Robert Church Park)
Possibly Robert Church, Sr., architect
1899/1920s
391 Beale

Robert R. Church, Sr., said to be the first African-American million-aire in the South, was born in 1839 to Captain Charles B. Church, a white steamboat captain. His early experiences were as a cabin boy on his father's boats during the 1850s. Around 1864 he opened a saloon at 29 Monroe Street. Church made his money in real estate and, in 1906, founded the Solvent Savings Bank and Trust Company (see building #50).

Church Park Auditorium (second version), 1940s. Its name was changed by the city in 1940 to "Beale Avenue Auditorium." This move infuriated the African-American community which petitioned the city to change it back. Success came in 1956.

In 1899 he built Church's Park and Auditorium on six acres of land for the Memphis black community. Beautifully landscaped with walks and flower beds, peacocks roamed freely throughout the park. A special feature was a round flower bed, 25 feet in diameter. A large banana tree stood in its center surrounded by rows of red cannas bordered by white periwinkles. Outdoor recreational facilities were available for children and, during the warmer months, fraternal bands and W. C. Handy's Orchestra played from the open-air band stand.

The major attraction, the auditorium, could seat 2000 in its theater. It also contained a large banquet hall underneath the stage. On 19 November

1902 President Theodore Roosevelt spoke in the auditorium to an audience of 10,000 which overflowed into the park. Booker T. Washington, during a tour of the state, was a guest speaker in 1909. Numerous conventions and meetings took place, including those of the Lincoln Republican League and the NAACP.

Many national theatrical troups, vaudeville acts, and touring orchestras made appearances, such as the Whitney Musical Company, the Smart Set with S. H. Dudley, famed opera singer Madame Sissieretta Jones (Black Patti), and the Fisk Jubilee Singers. Public dances were also held. During the big band era, the Jimmie Lunceford Orchestra was always booked at the Auditorium upon its return to Memphis. Lunceford had been a teacher at Manassas High School and formed his first band from among his students.

Church's son, Robert Church, Jr., also became an important businessman and political figure. He founded the Lincoln Republican League which strove to register black voters and also organized the first branch of the NAACP in Tennessee in 1917. As a powerful republican leader, Church was consulted by the national party on many occasions. In 1921 Church sold the park to the city for $85,000. They razed the original auditorium and built a new one (see photo). This also fell to the wrecking ball during the early 1970s. All that remains is a park established in the 1980s.

R. R. CHURCH,

 Buying, Renting and Selling of.... REAL ESTATE.

Office, 124 BEALE STREET.

Ad for Robert Church, real estate (current #: 318 Beale), 1899.

52. ELKS CLUB
(building demolished)
1908
401 Beale

The Improved Benevolent Protective Order of Elks of the World, black branch, was organized in Memphis on 26 June 1906. Around a year later, an injunction obtained by their white counterparts banned the group from the entire state of Tennessee. The injunction was lifted in 1937, mainly due to

Elks Club, 1970. Note the sign for "Elks Tropical Garden," which was actually part of Church Park.

the efforts of Robert Church, Jr. In 1938 the Elks moved into 403 Beale (later changed to number 401).

The Elks were one of several black fraternal orders in the city. Some of the others included: the Masons, Knights of Pythias, Knights of Tabor, Odd Fellows, Hotel Men's Improvement Club (for waiters), and the Chauffeur's Club. All of these organizations were civically and socially responsible. For example, the Elks donated a great amount of time and money to charity and food drives.

The Elks also advertised meeting rooms, dining, and dancing. Orchestras were frequently employed for proms and other social gatherings. During the 1940s, the Elks sponsored talent contests which included gospel groups, jug bands, dancers, and singers. Professional entertainers, such as B. B. King, Dwight "Gatemouth" Moore, and Rufus Thomas, also performed.

EYE, THROAT & LUNG DISEASES.
DR. CREIGHTON'S

Office Hours for these specialties are from 8 to 9 A. M. and from 3 to 6 P. M. Persons wishing Dr. CREIGHTON'S services must consult this arrangement.
Office in DRUG STORE, immediately opposite SOUTH MARKET, BEAL STREET.

Fee for Professional Visits, each $10.

Ad for Dr. Robert W. Creighton, physician and oculist (current #: 199 Beale), 1865.

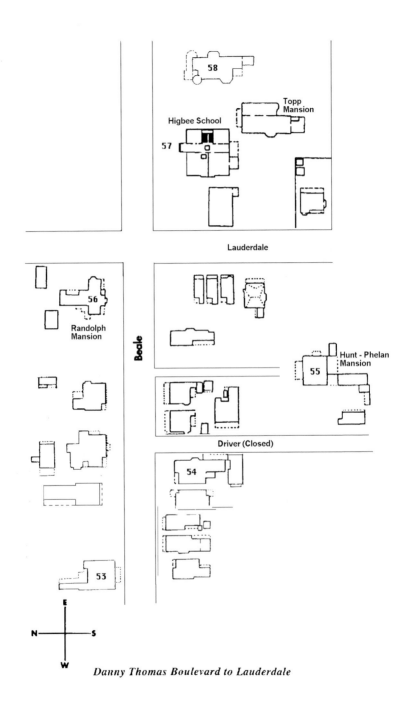

Danny Thomas Boulevard to Lauderdale

SECTION 6
DANNY THOMAS BOULEVARD
TO LAUDERDALE

53. THE PETTIT MANSION
(building removed)
1860
496 Beale

The Pettit Mansion, ca. 1937.

In 1846 Robertson Topp, Nathaniel Anderson, and William L. Vance, trustees of the South Memphis Company, auctioned off the remaining land in South Memphis. At the time this area, which included Beale Street, was a separate town from Memphis (see building #57). The lot, which eventually contained the Pettit home, was purchased by John A. Denie, a commission merchant. Denie nor any of the subsequent owners of the lot made any improvements until Robertson T. Torian.

Torian, an insurance agent who arrived in Memphis in 1857, bought the property in 1860 and began construction of a house which was completed the following year. In December 1865, H. A. Littleton, also an insurance agent, purchased the property. When Littleton resettled in Iowa, the house was sold to the Pettit Family in August 1876. They occupied it until 1937.

James T. Pettit moved to Memphis from Alabama in 1847. Originally in the dry goods business, Pettit became a planter and then after the Civil War, a cotton factor and commission merchant. After the Yellow Fever Epidemic of 1878, when Memphis lost its charter and became a taxing district of the state, Pettit was appointed to a committee to reorganize the city government. He was also President of the Chamber of Commerce and of the Memphis Cotton Exchange. In 1886, six years prior to his death, he became an officer of the Equitable Gaslight Company which made carbureted water gas. Hugh and William L. Pettit, both sons, were also in the cotton business.

This beautiful home, the photo of which was taken when its clapboards needed repairs and when pigeons roosted in its attic, was judged by the Department of the Interior in 1933 as an outstanding example of Southern architecture. They documented it thoroughly and placed a description and measurements of the home in the National Archives.

The fourteen room two-story house, built in the Greek Revival style, had four beautiful Ionic columns, each with a wrought-iron capital. Totally constructed in wood, its clapboards were of longleaf pine. The roof, imported from England, was unusual in being of hand-wrought iron dipped in lead. Attached to the rear of the house was a kitchen, smokehouse, and servants quarters.

The solid walnut front door was guarded by two sidelights made of red Venetian glass, each etched with a white floral pattern. Inside, every room was highlighted by a beautifully crafted frescoed pattern. The windows were fitted with full-length shutters, on movable slats, which opened into recessed panels. A central hallway cut through the house on both floors, separating three parlors and two dining rooms on the first and six bedrooms on the second. A semi-circular solid mahogany stairway with a rosewood banister swept up to the bedrooms. With the exception of the two baths, every room had a cast-iron fireplace finished in marble.

The home was dismantled by Mrs. George Wood Govert in 1939 who saved it from the wrecking ball. Her plan was to rebuild the house in Germantown, just outside Memphis. The extent of her endeavor deserves further investigation.

54. DR. RICHARD B. MAURY HOME
(Hunt-Phelan Home Visitor Center - original building demolished)
ca. 1892
513 Beale

Soon after the Battle of Memphis on 6 June 1862, as the population witnessed the defeat of the Confederate fleet just offshore, the Union army took control of the defenseless city. On June 23d General Ulysses S. Grant arrived in Memphis and appropriated the Hunt-Phelan Mansion for his headquarters (see building #55). Sometime earlier, William R. Hunt had taken his family, and much of their belongings, to Atlanta to assume command of the Confederate arsenal. Hunt had leased his house to McCaulty Aiken who was removed when Grant seized the home. Due to these circumstances, taxes on the mansion were not paid between the years 1862 and 1865.

The Dr. R. B. Maury Home, 1912.

With the return to normalcy and the family to its home, Hunt resumed his tax responsibilities. But his back taxes were not forgiven. Between 1869 and 1873, sections of the original Driver estate, on which the Hunt-Phelan home stood, were sold off to reduce the liability. The Hunt family retained one half with almost all of the remaining property going to Churchill J. Selden, past president of the Gayoso Savings Institution. Metellus L. Selden, Churchill's son, had married into the Hunt family and built a house on the property in 1870.

In 1871 Selden sold a 40 x 150 foot lot to Dr. Richard B. Maury on which he built a home in 1872. Around 1892 Dr. Maury purchased the lot next door and built a home which he rented out. This home may have been for his son, Richard, Jr., who died at the age of 30 in May of that year. He also had a new and larger structure built for himself. This is the house seen in the photograph.

Dr. Maury was born in 1834 in Georgetown, D. C. His father had been President Monroe's private secretary. Another relative was naval officer Matthew F. Maury who was responsible for the construction of the Memphis Navy Yard in the mid-1840s. He later became a distinguished United States Navy officer and a noted oceanographer.

Richard Maury received his medical degree from the University of Virginia and another one from New York University. Because of poor health, he was forced to relocate to a milder climate and in 1859 chose Port Gibson, Mississippi. During the Civil War, he worked as a surgeon for the Confederate army. In 1867 Dr. Maury moved to Memphis and opened a practice with Dr. Robert W. Mitchell near Court Square. He also taught at the Memphis Medical College.

Dr. Maury was an important leader in developing a hospital system in Memphis. Prior to the 1880s, hospitals were available only to travelers and the indigent and situated near the outskirts of town to protect residents from the dissemination of disease. City residents were treated in their homes. The development of a hospital system for local citizens was an attempt to better manage medical problems. In 1884 Maury opened an infirmary for women in which the first nurses in Memphis were trained. Later he helped to establish the Lucy Brinkley Hospital, the first institution of its kind in Memphis.

In 1877 Dr. Maury became the first representative in West Tennessee of the newly founded Tennessee Department of Public Health. During his tenure, he argued for sanitary and preventative public health measures, such as the use of quarantines when necessary. Dr. Maury was also president of the Board of Education and the founder of the West Tennessee Audubon Society. He died in 1919. A son, Dr. J. M. Maury, was also a noted physician.

55. THE HUNT-PHELAN MANSION
Robert Mills, architect
ca.1842-1857
533 Beale

The Hunt-Phelan Mansion, 1935. A two-story porch, which protrudes from the center of the house, separates the original portion at the left from additions made in 1850. The window bay on the porch was added much later, probably in the 1960s.

Around 1842 George H. Wyatt built the house which was to become the Hunt-Phelan Mansion. Of all the magnificent homes which once dominated this residential area, it is the only one to survive the ravages of urban renewal.

A land surveyor and an engineer, Wyatt arrived in Memphis from Virginia sometime in the early 1830s. The Shelby County Circuit Court called him for jury duty in June 1835, the first such documentation of his residence in Memphis. As early as 1835, he bought and sold land in the Memphis area. Some of these purchases were for the construction of the LaGrange and Memphis Railroad of which Wyatt was a commissioner. This was the first railroad initiative in Memphis but failed in 1843, with only six miles of track laid, due to lack of financing. In 1836 Wyatt also formed a partnership with Lewis Trezevant where they sold dry goods, groceries, and hardware out of a store next to the Farmers and Merchants Bank on the corner of Main and Winchester.

In 1837 Wyatt moved to Marshall County, Mississippi, just four miles south of LaGrange, Tennessee. Here he operated a plantation which had, in 1840, ninety-one slaves. In 1839 Wyatt opened a private female academy at his home with room enough to board up to twelve students. The five-year course of study in liberal arts was supported by his personal library which included many books on such subjects as geology, botany, chemistry, math, history, and philosophy. Wyatt moved back to Memphis in the early 1840s, perhaps because of his affiliation with the LaGrange and Memphis Railroad.

Wyatt also may have been a shareholder of the South Memphis Company, headed by Robertson Topp, which was entrusted with the land that eventually became the town of South Memphis (see building #57). Shareholders could exchange their stock for lots and this may have been the way Wyatt came to build a house on 5 $^{77}/_{100}$ acres on the corner of Beale and Lauderdale. Apparently, the South Memphis Company still owned the lot. When Wyatt ran into financial problems he paid $1300 to the company which transferred the property to the Union Bank on 9 August 1845. In December Jesse M. Tate, a cousin, bought the property from the bank for $7000. In the meantime, Wyatt headed west to find his fortune in the California gold rush. After his wife died in 1851, he entrusted his children to a guardian.

In July 1850 Colonel Eli M. Driver, another cousin, purchased the property from Tate for $8250. Colonel Driver, a land commissioner, had extensive real estate holdings which were estimated to be worth $225,000 in 1850. Driver maintained a large number of slaves who worked as house servants and as field hands on his cotton plantations in Tunica County, Mississippi.

Colonel Driver's daughter, Sarah Elizabeth, married Colonel William R. Hunt who took possession of the house in 1851 after Driver's death due to consumption. Six generations of the Hunt family and their descendants, the Phelans, have lived in the mansion.

The property originally included a smokehouse, barns, stables, and slave cabins. The long tree-lined driveway brought visitors in full view of a striking brick house sitting in a grove of magnolias. Its two-stories, each balanced with four rooms and a central hallway, eyed the beautiful gardens and grounds through windows crowned with stone lintels. Guests stepped from their carriages to face a handsome front entrance with a wide, square transom over the door and two strips of narrow side lights. Built in the Federal style, the house was and still is an impressive sight.

In 1850 Colonel Driver added a two-story kitchen at the rear which contained servants quarters, a laundry room, a repair shop, and a wood storage area. A two-story porch joined it to the main house. Colonel Driver also left orders in his will that the small Dorian portico over the front entrance be moved to the side entryway. A much larger portico, in Greek Revival style, was to replace it. When these changes were made around 1857, four channeled Ionic wood columns were added to the larger portico, each having a cast-iron base and cap to support its wooden roof.

In July 1861, Confederate General Leonidas Polk, a friend of Colonel Hunt, stayed at the house to organize the Army of Tennessee and to plan the defense of the Mississippi River. Jefferson Davis, another personal friend, assigned Hunt to command the arsenal at Atlanta which was later moved to Selma, Alabama. After Memphis fell to Union forces on 6 June 1862, General Ulysses S. Grant appropriated the house for his headquarters, where he may have planned the second Battle of Vicksburg in its library.

After Grant left, the house and grounds were heavily fortified against raids by General Nathan Bedford Forrest. In building trenches and camouflaging key positions, Union troops tore down most of the structures surrounding the residence. They also enlarged and lengthened a tunnel originally built under the center of the house by George Wyatt for food storage. The new tunnel, now used for the transport of soldiers and dispatches, stretched across Beale Street to another house.

On a foggy morning in 1864, Forrest's Raiders attacked Memphis. Their goal was to capture key Union commanders, but they were only partly successful. Riding up Lauderdale Street, his cavalry fired a rifle barrage at the house which scared the daylights out of the Union officers living there.

In February 1863, the house was turned into a hospital and kind of USO operated by the Western Sanitary Commission. Called the Soldiers Home, it cared for thousands of Union troops. During the war, the Freedmen's Bureau built a schoolhouse for newly liberated slaves which still stands, shriveled and dilapidated, just behind the French gardens at the rear of the house.

In 1993 Stephen R. Phelan died, the last member of the family to live in the house. His cousin, William Day, placed the house under a foundation. After renovation, the house opened as a museum in 1996. Remarkably, the family never threw anything out. The contents of the home include: antebellum furniture, a rare 1859 Steinway grand piano, a library of around 3000 antique books, correspondence from President Andrew Johnson, Jefferson Davis, and General Nathan Bedford Forrest, among others, and two previously unknown photographs of Jefferson Davis. All of this adds considerably to the significance of the house and to the history of Beale Street.

56. THE WILLIAM M. RANDOLPH MANSION
(building demolished)
1875
546 Beale

The William M. Randolph Mansion, 1912.

The series of events which led to the sale of the lot upon which William M. Randolph eventually built his mansion reads like a stupefying soap opera of real estate conveyances. It involved several principals, including John C. Parker and Charles Jones. Parker, who at various times was a banker, cotton dealer, distiller, and whiskey dealer, bought this property in 1867. In 1866 he also was involved in the development of Rawlings Place (which later became an extension of Pontotoc Street) near Lauderdale and Vance, two blocks south of Beale.

From the beginning, Parker had financial difficulties and neglected to pay his property taxes. He also owed Charles Jones, a contractor and builder, for work and materials furnished for the construction of a dwelling on the property. Jones to get his money, became a litigant in a court case between Benjamin May, the cashier at the Bank of West Tennessee, and T. S. Ayers, Parker's lawyer. The case involved the same property owned by Parker. Litigation began in 1868 and ended in the early part of 1874.

After Parker moved to St. Louis, he sold the property to William M. Randolph on 26 January 1874 for only $5.00. In exchange Randolph may have settled some of Parker's debts. He did pay all of the property taxes on the lot going back to 1867, amounting to around $1200. Randolph probably began construction of his mansion, a superb example of Italian Renaissance architecture, in 1874. After the purchase of additional property, by the late 1800s the Randolph estate stood on a lot measuring 210 x 244 feet.

Randolph, born in LaGrange, Tennessee, had a large law practice in Little Rock, Arkansas, before the Civil War. After moving to Memphis in 1865, he was city attorney from 1869 until 1874 and afterwards a judge. He built the Randolph Office Building in 1891 (see building #3).

In 1885 Randolph, in the U. S. Circuit Court, argued unsuccessfully in support of a black woman to sit anywhere she wished on a train (*Logwood v. Memphis & Charleston Railroad,* 23 Fed. Rep. 318). The decision upheld the constitutionality of the Alabama statute for the separation of the two races upon public conveyances. It was one of many cases cited by the U. S. Supreme Court to support their conclusion that the East Louisiana Railroad could sit customers where they pleased as long as the seats were of equal quality. This 1896 decision (*Plessy v. Ferguson,* 163 US 537) upheld several state statutes and established a national policy of separate but equal facilities.

Randolph's Italianate house looked like four homes in one. The entire structure was asymmetrical with an off-center square tower which silently guarded the entranceway. The section to its right contained a massive bay window supported by a concrete pedestal. With its rounded arched windows, pilasters, corbels, ornate roof brackets, and beautifully embellished interior woodwork, the house was listed in The National Register of Historic Places. However, general neglect, a fire, excessive vandalism, and an inability to secure restoration funds led to its demolition in 1976. What remains is one out building and a brick border covered in concrete which once supported a wrought-iron fence.

57. THE ROBERTSON TOPP MANSION/THE HIGBEE
SCHOOL FOR GIRLS
(Memphis Technical Assistance & Resource Center -
original buildings demolished)
1837-1841/1887
565 Beale

The Robertson Topp Mansion, ca. 1938.

Robertson Topp, an important figure in the development of Memphis, was a lawyer and head of the South Memphis Company which acted as trustee for 470 acres of land, including the original Fearn tract of 414 acres. This area, which contained Beale Street and lay south of Union Avenue (the dividing line was the middle of the street), became incorporated as the town of South Memphis in 1846. It merged with Memphis in 1850.

An energetic and dynamic man, Topp built the Gayoso Hotel in 1842 and became president of the Memphis and Ohio Railroad. He also served fourteen years in the Tennessee legislature for the Whig party. A visionary, he foresaw Memphis as an important commercial center and as a crossroads for railroad transportation in the Mid-South.

Robertson Topp, probably late 1830s, when he was a member of the Tennessee legislature. This is the only known image of Topp and is most likely a painting, not a photograph.

A Unionist, Topp opposed secession which he felt would have destroyed the future of Memphis and bring great disaster to the South. After Abraham Lincoln was elected, Topp was asked to be on his cabinet but he declined. He also refused an offer from President Jefferson Davis for a commission as a general in the Confederate army, although he eventually joined the Southern cause. With his real estate holdings valued at $620,000 in 1860, the aftermath of the war found his fortunes reversed. He returned to Memphis to find his home being used as a warehouse. With some resentment, from the end of the war until his death in 1876, Topp tried unsuccessfully to sue the Federal government for cotton seized and appropriated from him and others. He valued his share at one million dollars.

Topp, during his tenure on the state legislature in Nashville, married Elizabeth L. Vance in April 1837. Upon their return to Memphis, they began construction of a home at this location which was completed in 1841. As of 1840 Topp and an associate, Thomas B. Haralson, were the only residents of the huge tract of land referred to as South Memphis. The Topp mansion originally stood on fifteen acres of land, set 150 feet back from Beale. In the 1840s the view was limited to the Hunt-Phelan home (building #55) and a thick grove of trees. The two mansions matched each other in palatial beauty.

Built in the Greek Revival style, the front of the Topp residence had four Corinthian columns, supporting a dentilled pediment. This ornamentation extended around the house at the cornice. The hand carved front door opened into a rotunda which, in turn, led into a hallway. All the doors, in fact, were similarly crafted as were the solid mahogany semi-circular stairway and some of the built-in cabinets. The keys to these fourteen foot high doors were eight inches long and made of solid silver. Topp imported marble fireplace mantles from Italy, as well as the workmen who were to fresco the ceilings exactly as in the rooms where the fireplaces were originally placed. He also imported rosewood furniture and french mirrors. All the windows on the first floor reached from the floor to the ceiling, except for the bay window at the rear of the house which overlooked the gardens through hand-blown curved glass. The living quarters were on the second floor and on a third floor which may have originally been an attic. Altogether there were about twenty rooms.

In 1861, at a cost of $40,000, Topp hired Cincinnati architect James B. Cook to remodel the house. Some of the walls were hand painted and new hardwood woodwork and silver plated door knobs and hinges were added. A beautiful side porch with a balcony may have been constructed at this time. The house was torn down in 1939.

The belief still persists that at least one location in Memphis was part of The Underground Railroad, the secretive organization pledged to hide runaway slaves until they could be safely transported north across the Ohio River. Sam Shankman and Annie Mayhew, in conversations with individuals at the Higbee School (see below) during the 1910s, including a black gardener whose father and grandfather were slaves of Robertson Topp, suggest that the Topp residence was used for runaway slaves. A secret passage was discovered in the wainscoting of one of the rooms in which a spring released a section of the baseboard. Inside could be seen clothing fragments and rusted tin utensils. It was surmised that the bayou which crossed part of the Topp residence would have been used by escaping slaves.

Robertson Topp was a man torn between two political worlds. A staunch Unionist, he did not favor secession but he also owned several cotton plantations and hundreds of slaves. Whether he was a kind of "Schindler" is unknown but it may be that his belief in slavery changed over the years. If the house was part of The Underground Railroad, it is most likely that this occurred during the Civil War before Union troops occupied the city in 1862. Since the house no longer stands, archaeological evidence suffers, but the search for further documentation certainly deserves serious attention.

The Higbee School for Girls, 1895.

Jennie M. Higbee arrived in Memphis from New Jersey shortly after the Civil War. She established a small school and from there became principal of the city high school. In 1880 she purchased the Robertson Topp Mansion and opened a finishing school for young girls whose families could be counted among the upper crust of society.

A new building was constructed a few years later and the Topp Mansion was relegated to a dormitory. The school operated until 1914. The building remained vacant for several years, until 1920, when it became the offices of the Tribe of Ben Hur, a fraternal society. Its last occupant, from 1924 until it was torn down in the 1970s, was the Labor Temple. At one time, the facility contained the headquarters for over 50 different unions.

58. THE JOHN F. HOLST MANSION
(building demolished)
1888
583 Beale

Christian K. Holst arrived in Boston from Denmark sometime before 1833 where he married the Irish-born Margaret Hindman. With three young sons, the family moved to Kentucky and then to Memphis in 1843. Christian was a cabinet maker and upholsterer but at some undetermined time, he also became an undertaker. This aspect of his business became dominant during the mid-1850s until it remained as the family's sole enterprise. For most of the nearly seventy years they were in business, their establishment stood on the east side of Main Street between Union and Monroe.

The John F. Holst Mansion, 1912.

After Christian died in 1862, at the age of sixty-two, the business fell to his oldest son Julius who, with his brothers George and Theodore, operated it as "Julius C. Holst and Company, undertakers." When Julius died in 1872, at the age of thirty-eight, the business went to George, the next oldest, who ran it with Theodore until 1878. That year the worst of three yellow fever epidemics during the 1870s hit Memphis. The Holsts, like many other well-to-do citizens, could have left the city but, as funeral directors, they chose to stay and face the responsibility of their business which had reached an almost insurmountable level of demand. Within three weeks of each other, during the month of September, both brothers succumbed to the disease. Their brother-in-law, James Ward, also became a victim. Their mother and George's widow continued to operate the firm.

John F. Holst, the youngest son, did not have an interest in the business. He initially worked as a salesman with his brother-in-law, James Ward, at Garthwaite, Lewis and Stuart, a men's clothing store. When Ward set up his own men's clothing business in 1869, Holst became a bookeeper until Ward's death in 1878. At that point, with the death of his brothers and Ward, Holst became manager of the undertaking firm. In 1882 he received a raise to $125 per month. The next year he bought out his mother's share of the business and, in 1884, he paid $10,000 to George's widow. J. F. Holst and Brother stayed in business until around 1916 when Holst retired and sold it to Jesse T. Hinton who had been a partner since the late 1890s. Holst died in 1921, one month after a niece. The undertaking business must have been pretty good. On his death certificate, Mrs. Holst listed "Capitalist" as her husband's occupation.

For many years the family lived on Main Street over their business. In 1867 Julius bought a lot on Beale Street next to the Pettit home (building #53) and built a mansion for his mother, siblings, and the Ward Family, although he and Theodore continued to reside at the Main Street address. After the death of his brothers, John assumed the leadership of the family. In 1888 he purchased a lot from the Topp Estate and built a house just west of the Robertson Topp Mansion (building #57). His mother and sister, Mrs. Maria J. Ward, built a home across the street which was similar in design but smaller in size.

John Holst's home is shown in the photo. The first floor, constructed of stone, had a mammoth arched entranceway which supported a balcony on the second floor. The spectacular wrap-around porch at the left offset a three-story tower topped by a cone-shaped roof on the right. In 1916, when Holst retired, he sold his Beale Street residence and moved to another mansion at 243 S. Belvedere Boulevard which still stands.

In the early 1940s, the Beale home became the offices of the Construction and General Laborers Local Union #1441. The house was demolished in the late 1960s.

BEALE STREET BUSINESS DIRECTORY

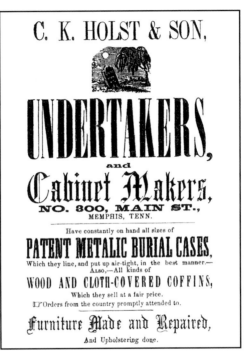

C. K. HOLST & SON,

UNDERTAKERS,

and

Cabinet Makers,

NO. 800, MAIN ST.,
MEMPHIS, TENN.

Have constantly on hand all sizes of

PATENT METALIC BURIAL CASES,

Which they line, and put up air-tight, in the best manner.—
ALSO,—All kinds of

WOOD AND CLOTH-COVERED COFFINS,

Which they sell at a fair price.
☞ Orders from the country promptly attended to.

Furniture Made and Repaired,

And Upholstering done.

Ad for C. K. Holst Undertakers, 1854.

W. H. WALKER,

✧ TAILOR. ✧

Cutting, Cleaning, Dyeing and Repairing.

No. 141 BEALE ST., MEMPHIS, TENN.

A full assortment of Samples of the Latest Styles of Goods kept on hand.
All Work Promptly and Neatly Done.

Ad for W. H. Walker, tailor (current #: 341 Beale), 1882.

Ad for The Moon, a weekly African-American Magazine, 1906.

Ad for Mariani's Exchange, saloon (current #: 350 Beale), 1899.

Ad for Hetzel and Company (current #: 601 Beale), 1866.

Ad for Lorenzo Pacini (P. Wee's, 317 Beale), 1899.

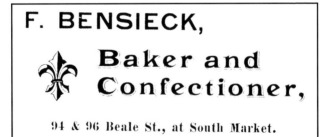

Ad for Frank Bensieck, baker (current #: 182-184 Beale), 1899.

INDEX

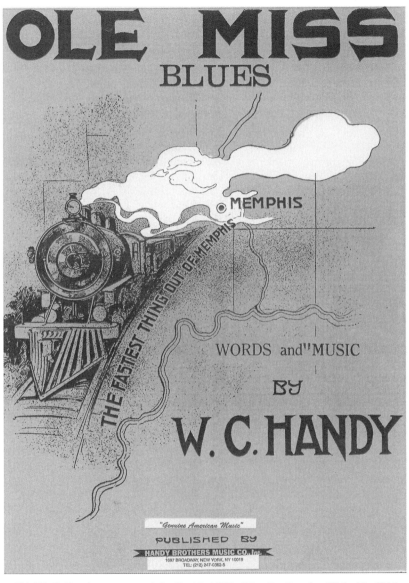

This W. C. Handy tune was originally titled "Ole Miss Rag" and published in 1916.